W9-BAX-704

God's Peculiar People

God's Peculiar People

Women's Voices & Folk Tradition in a Pentecostal Church

ELAINE J. LAWLESS

THE UNIVERSITY PRESS OF KENTUCKY

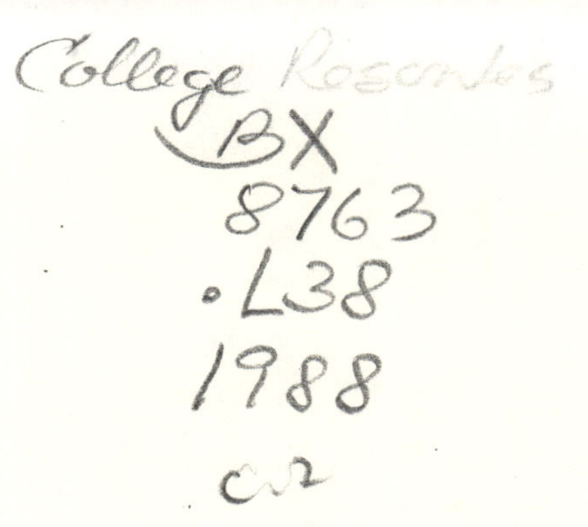

Scholarly publisher for the Commonwealth,
serving Bellarmine College, Berea College, Centre
College of Kentucky, Eastern Kentucky University,
The Filson Club, Georgetown College, Kentucky
Historical Society, Kentucky State University,
Morehead State University, Murray State University,
Northern Kentucky University, Transylvania University,
University of Kentucky, University of Louisville,
and Western Kentucky University.

Editorial and Sales Offices: Lexington, Kentucky 40506-0336

Library of Congress Cataloging-in-Publication Data

Lawless, Elaine J.
God's peculiar people: women's voices & folk tradition in a Pentecostal church / Elaine J. Lawless.
p. cm.
Bibliography: p.
Includes index.
ISBN 0-8131-1628-7
1. Oneness Pentecostal churches—Indiana—Monroe County.
2. Oneness Pentecostal churches—Indiana—Lawrence County.
3. Monroe County (Ind.)—Church history. 4. Lawrence County (Ind.)—Church history. 5. Women, Pentecostal—Indiana—Monroe County.
6. Women, Pentecostal—Indiana—Lawrence County. I. Title.
BX8763.L38 1988
289.9'4'09772255—dc 19 88-4236

This book is printed on acid-free paper meeting
the requirements of the American National Standard
for Permanence of Paper for Printed Library Materials. ♾

Contents

To my parents
James Harold Lawless
and Angie Mae Dunlap Lawless

Acknowledgments

I would like to thank Mary Ellen Brown and Richard Bauman at Indiana University, Larry Danielson at the University of Illinois, Bill Clements at Arkansas State, William Wilson at Brigham Young University, and Mary Lago at the University of Missouri for their constant and continued support and encouragement of my work. Many members of the American Folklore Society have helped me as well with their comments and critiques of much of this material at the annual American Folklore Society Meetings. I especially want to acknowledge the importance of Betsy Peterson as my fellow fieldworker for many of the trips that formed the basis for this book, and as a friend. My work in this area since working with her in Indiana has suffered the loss of her perception, intelligence and wit. Finally, I want to thank Sandy Rikoon for his loving encouragement, his unerring confidence in me, and his tolerance when I forget to be mellow; and Alex and Jesse for being wonderful, patient, and beautiful kids, even when they couldn't quite figure out why Mom had to go to church so often.

Portions of some of the chapters in this book appeared in different form in scholarly journals. I wish to thank the *Journal of American Folklore*, *Western Folklore*, and *Southern Folklore Quarterly* for their permission to include this material here.

Looking for that blessed hope, and the glorious appearing of the great God and our Savior Jesus Christ; Who gave himself for us, that he might redeem us from all iniquity, and purify unto himself a peculiar people, zealous of good works.

—*Titus 2:13-14*

You know, when I sing
And when I testify
Everybody looks at me
And they think I'm kind of
Peculiar.
But you know tonight
We are peculiar people.

—from a Pentecostal woman's testimony

Preface

God has a hand in whatever we do. Whatever we do down the line, He sees that we make it. And if you serve God, you'll make it![1]

This book is a study of some of the traditional religious practices of a particular Pentecostal sect, the "Jesus Only" or "Oneness" Pentecostals, so-named because they believe God the Father and Jesus the Son are one and the same. For believers of this group and for other Pentecostals, this means they are not considered to be a trinitarian religious denomination. The most distinctive feature of their religious point of view is manifested by their baptism ritual. Whereas all trinitarian Christians baptize in "the name of the Father, the Son, and the Holy Ghost," this group baptizes only "in the name of Jesus." Such a deviation from standard Christian ritual has, indeed, caused controversy to surround this Pentecostal sect. Pentecostals in general have drawn attention to themselves since the birth of this twentieth-century American denomination.[2] Their charismatic religious gatherings, which focus on the possession of the Holy Spirit and the accompanying tongue-speaking, shouting, and "falling out" behaviors have received both widespread attention and derision.[3] Pentecostals, and to an even greater degree Oneness Pentecostals, recognize that they are viewed as a "peculiar people," but their gritty response has been to mark that distinction with pride: "we are peculiar people and we are proud of it!"

Oneness Pentecostalism currently represents a strong and growing segment of religious people, especially in the southern portions of the states considered to be part of the Upland South; this study focuses mainly on one group in southern Indiana.[4] The approach of this book is not historical, nor is it psychological, although some history of the group is presented in order to place this particular group of Pentecostals in historical context and some psychological functions of religious traditions are discussed in a detailed examination of women's testimonies. The study is not an anthropological one, although the "ethnography of speaking" approach to traditional verbal genres stems from the work of anthropologist Dell Hymes and others interested in documentation of context.[5]

This study is unique in that it is an ethnographic examination of the religious traditions of one congregation. The hope is that close investigation of one congregation can help us to better understand the larger religious picture. There is no single thing that *all* Pentecostals do, but how they choose to combine the traditional elements available to them does result in an identifiable package we recognize as "Pentecostal." The traditions examined here include group attitudes Pentecostals hold about themselves as well as those they hold about outsiders; rules about personal behavior and dress; and religious practices both within the church service context and beyond it.

As a folklorist, I am looking at this oral religious context as a traditional one—that is, a world view and a set of beliefs and rituals passed from generation to generation and from group member to group member in an oral fashion. The various religious verbal genres performed during each service are excellent extant examples of oral, traditional art.[6] Within the context of one church, even within the context of one service, we are able to discern how the oral, traditional process operates. None of the verbal genres performed in this context have ever been written down before; they are created spontaneously and performed orally within a strong tradition that dictates performance form and style and are evaluated by a competent, critical audience of peer believers. The traditional genres performed at each service include singing, praying, testifying, healing, preaching, and speaking in tongues. All of these genres will be placed in the context of the service as a whole, and the final chapter of this book will focus entirely on the testimony as one significant religious verbal genre capable of altering status quo equations within the context of the religious service.

There is a bias in this book toward the experience of Pentecostal women. This bias is intended but not forced. My fieldwork both in southern Indiana and, currently, in southern Missouri, indicates that significantly more women than men are involved in this charismatic religion. Not only do more women attend these churches, but they participate in the services in greater numbers and with more intensity,[7] because this religious arena is approved as a forum for free participation in emotional religious response and ecstacy. Because historically women in this country have not had many such forums available to them, it is understandable that where their participation is condoned they take full advantage of the opportunity to speak and to perform.

Fieldwork for this study of Pentecostals in Monroe and Lawrence counties in southern Indiana began in 1977 after I had conducted a field collection of personal experience narratives from white women in the area who were wives, mothers, and sisters of men who worked in the limestone quarries that dominate the landscape of southern Indiana. I identified a corpus of "disaster stories" that were told and retold—stories that exhibited the women's sense of helplessness in the face of ever-impending disaster at the quarries, danger that often maimed or killed their menfolk. I became acquainted with women who were extremely fatalistic, yet deeply religious. All power for safety was in God's hands; whatever He did was for a reason. The best way they had found for coping with the insecurities of their lives was to go to church and pray to God to take care of them and their families and pray that their menfolk would get into the church "before it's too late." I began to go to church with them, curious about the Pentecostal faith, which obviously meant so much to them and had such a direct influence on their daily lives. A few services were enough to indicate the rich store of folklore material in every aspect of this strictly fundamentalist religion—from dress codes, church rituals, codes of interaction, to the belief system. The fieldwork was exciting because I knew I was stepping into a long-ignored and misunderstood field, that of rural fundamentalist religious beliefs and practices.[8]

Fieldwork with Pentecostals over the past several years has yielded hours of both audio and video tape, which includes religious services and interviews with church members. It is certainly true that a recorder cannot capture everything, but I disagree with the notion that the tape recorder disrupts the services and that analyses can be based on memory alone. Verbatim transcripts have been invaluable in this study and should form the basis of any study of folklore traditions. As a supplement to the tape recordings of services, in my fieldwork I always keep a journal in which I note specifics such as the number in attendance, sex, age, evidence of economic status; the location of the church; and my personal impressions of particular services or people. The tapes capture, of course, only the verbal components of the services, and it is always vitally important to note at the same time the paralinguistic and semiotic elements involved. I often sketch seating arrangements and note the regular attenders; record who participates most, both physically and verbally—who raises hands, cries, dances, sings, and prays. I like to check the responses of visitors; I note the attitudes of the attending children. I am also interested in how the members talk to me and to each other before and after church—that is, how do they frame the church experience?

My fieldwork in Pentecostal churches developed in three rather distinct phases. At first, I attended the churches to which I was invited by my neighbor friends—small, rural churches nearly all of which were within five miles of Bloomington. The second phase was of several months' duration and was concentrated in one small rural church nearly thirty miles south of Bloomington. The third phase, also extending over several months, was conducted at a church in Bloomington.

In the winter of 1978, I began to attend several Pentecostal churches in southern Indiana on a regular basis. Typical of these was a tiny church whose services were conducted in the converted front room of the pastor's house. The congregation was composed of about fifteen women; the only males in attendance were the pastor, who was old and ailing, his younger son who drove down from Indianapolis to hold regular services, and a few of the small children. Many of my first impressions about Pentecostalism were formed in that tiny building. Since the congregation was composed entirely of women, it was the women who led the singing, prayed, testified, and spoke in tongues; the men preached and healed the women. This pattern has persisted in nearly every Pentecostal church I have ever attended, although most congregations have some male members.

The second phase of my field research grew out of a personal concern about how little most people know about Pentecostalism. From my childhood I remembered my parents talking of the "Holy Rollers" in our area of southern Missouri and my father's particular aversion to a Pentecostal boyfriend of mine. Most attitudes about Pentecostals were rooted in ignorance and in discomfort about the noise that could be heard for miles on warm summer nights through the open doors and windows of the little Pentecostal churches, which seemed to appear overnight on the dirt roads between the cotton fields in that part of the country. There were many Pentecostal churches, both black and white, and they were feared and misunderstood more than hated.

Concerned about the fears and ignorance that surround most non-Pentecostal attitudes toward Pentecostals, another folklorist, Elizabeth Peterson, and I set about to make a videotape on Pentecostals in southern Indiana. Our videotape, *Joy Unspeakable,* intended for social agencies and educators, was developed to promote understanding and improve the interactions of these agencies with the large number of Pentecostals with whom they worked daily and of whom they knew so little.[9] The fieldwork for this project took us to numerous Pentecostal churches in southern Indiana. For nearly a year we regularly attended several Pentecostal churches, and the patterns of ritual behavior we found were similar to those I had already observed. It was during this time that the important differences between trinitarian and Oneness Pentecostals became more apparent to us.

In preparation for the eventual videotape, we did extensive fieldwork with one small church at the edge of a particularly economically depressed town nearly thirty miles from Bloomington. This church has a congregation of twenty to twenty-five regular attenders, predominantly women, and has two pastors, one the son of the previous long-time pastor and the other a younger man who drives nearly forty miles for every service to co-pastor the church. This younger pastor's wife is also an ordained preacher in the Apostolic Church of Jesus Christ, Inc., one of many independent Oneness congregations. She is not, however, one of the pastors of the church; rather, she considers herself an evangelist. Within the Oneness Pentecostal tradition, it appears that this is a general pattern: women are allowed to be preachers but they are rarely, if ever, granted a pastorate.

This church never consented to our videotaping one of their services, fearing that we were unwittingly part of the Antichrist and that their doors would be marked and persecution would follow. But we were allowed to tape all services; most of the transcripts included in this study are from this church, identified here as Johnson's Creek Church. Months of regular attendance convinced the church of our sincerity, if not our willingness to yield to the Lord and join their ranks.

The argument for extended fieldwork with one folk group is a sound one. During the course of our work with this one church, we learned every regular member's name and relationship to every other member in the congregation. I can still recognize a member's voice on the tapes. We interviewed many of the members of this congregation and regularly visited some who became our friends. Our friendship was coveted, and our subsequent withdrawal from this field situation has created a sense of loss both for them and for us. At times, the imbalance between our knowledge of their lives and their knowledge of ours led me to feel the exploitative possibilities of such a study. I recall the words of James Agee in *Let Us Now Praise Famous Men*: "It seems to me curious, not to say obscene and thoroughly terrifying, that it could occur to an association of human beings . . .to pry intimately into the lives of an undefended . . . group of human beings for the purpose of parading the nakedness, disadvantage and humiliation of these lives before another group of human beings."[10]

The third phase of fieldwork with Pentecostals began in the summer of 1980 with a Pentecostal Assembly in Bloomington, Indiana. This congregation was the first racially mixed congregation we had encountered; a campus-oriented church, it draws blacks and foreign students into its doors as well as a long-standing group of local members, several of whom retain some connection with the local limestone industry. It also boasted a larger male population than any other church we had studied. Nevertheless, close attention to tape recordings of services at this church yielded the same general pattern of male-female participation as the other churches in this area. The pastor is a man, and there are several strong women in this congregation who testify and, in general, set the tenor of the services. After several months of tape recording services at this church, we were allowed to videotape a gospel-rock concert, a regular Sunday evening service, and a camp-meeting revival.

Field recordings of Pentecostal church services have been supplemented by interviews with members of the congregation. I wished to meet believers in their homes and make them more comfortable with the role I was taking in their religious rituals; I needed to have the church members explain the various facets of the church services to me to help me understand what I had heard and seen; and I wanted the believers to explain in their own words what the Pentecostal experience meant to them. Nearly all of the interviews I conducted were successful in terms of one or all of these intended goals. But the interviews often began awkwardly; eliciting conversation about religious beliefs is often troublesome and even painful, sometimes for both parties. Suspicion has not always been dissipated and in nearly every interview situation believers took the opportunity to "witness" to me and try to make me believe. My constricted behavior at their church services often became the focus of conversation, and I would be chastised for my reluctance to "let go" and "get into" the services. We nearly always knelt to pray before I departed.

Often in Pentecostal services the visitor is the only suspected sinner in the familiar congregation, and the efforts of both the preacher and the congregation become focused on converting the newcomer. I am aware that many sermons have been preached to me. This is not to say, however, that such a situation leaves the needs of the members unattended. In fact, just the opposite occurs. The members desire above all to "receive a blessing" and participate in an enthusiastic service; deadpan services rarely bring forth showers of blessings. Having a sinner in their midst upon whom to focus the intensity of their convictions actually enhances enthusiasm; testimonies to God's goodness and mercy that fall on the ears of a sinner ought to be even more convincing than those shared only with fellow believers, who do not necessarily need to be convinced, just uplifted. A preacher who has a sinner to preach to preaches differently from one addressing his faithful flock. And his fervor is contagious; all share the desire to see the lost one accept the invitation and encounter that ultimately exciting first experience of receiving the Holy Ghost and speaking in tongues. All join in the effort to convince; their displays become testimonials to their faith and the atmosphere becomes charged. Whether or not the visitor actually joins in, the mere presence of a nonmember serves to intensify the situation and stimulate the congregation.

The fieldworker in this situation is often not prepared for the concentrated attentions of the church members. The visitor is encouraged to join in all the activities from singing to dancing around the pews. At the end of the service, a member may even take the hand of the newcomer in an effort to urge her or him to come to the altar at the front of the church. But it is important to understand that it is acceptable merely to state that one doesn't "feel it" or that one is "not ready." After a certain point, the concentration on the visitor lessens as the members get "caught up in the spirit." Believers will be the first to say that acting without the spirit is blasphemous and that God may not be "dealing with" the sinner, but prolonged refusal to participate becomes frustrating for the believers and eventually the visitor may be seen as rejecting the spirit of God and suffer the suspicions of the congregation.

In the fieldwork situation, I always try to identify myself as an academic interested in Pentecostal religion, belief, and practice, not from a personal, experiential point of view but as a scholarly endeavor. I try to assure the believers that I am not a curiosity seeker, that I have not come to ridicule their behavior, but that I have come to learn, partly in the hope of helping to dispel stereotypes and misunderstandings about their religion. I insist that I must remain a nonmember in order to ensure objectivity. For a time, this attitude is generally accepted, and most of the members become accustomed to seeing me in their midst. During these services body language becomes of paramount importance; even so simple a sign as eye contact with the preacher during the altar call can convey the mistaken message "help me" or "I'm ready—urge me just a little." As the firmness of my stance becomes apparent, the attempts to convert me become somewhat more subtle, but they never completely disappear as the consensus of the congregation now becomes solidified: the shared challenge is to convince the scholar of the truth of the Pentecostal experience. What better testament to God and his power than the conversion of one who has merely come to study and observe? Several Pentecostals have openly expressed this attitude to me. They profess to be concerned for my soul; God did not send me to them to study Pentecostalism, but He has led me to them to expose me to his word and lead me to the "true experience." It is their duty to undertake the challenge. As a fieldworker, I have attempted to meet this attitude with gratitude for their concern and for their continued tolerance of me in their midst.

Although I am aware that my presence in many of the smaller services may alter the dynamics of the services, my long-term fieldwork in so many different church contexts and situations has convinced me that I can speak with confidence about what typically happens in Pentecostal church services. The folklorist can never be certain what happens when she is not around, but extensive fieldwork in the same area yields a consistent, reliable body of data, valuable in its own right.

The particularized details that pertain to Johnson's Creek Church in this study are simultaneously unique to one congregation and representative of the Pentecostal experience in general. Although the people in this study are certainly literate and operate within a world of print and media, their religous world is an oral one. The traditions, customs, and religious practices are developed and fostered within their religious milieu, whether in their own small churches or at revivals and camp meetings. Theirs is a folk religious community.

Introduction

Now, my parents didn't go to Bible College. Neither did me or my husband. The knowing that we have, our ministry, just comes from the Lord and just daily prayer and studying on our own. So, it's a lot different from other denominations. You can see that already.

IN MANY respects, the study of American folk religious traditions is still in an embryonic stage. It is unfortunate that such an expressive part of our culture is often ignored, even avoided. But many people feel uncomfortable examining the specifics of religions of their own culture too closely, and many scholars feel trepidation when they find themselves in a religious context unfamiliar to them, especially one that is strongly evangelical and prone to proselytizing, urging not only participation but conversion as well. It seems easier for us to study the Amish, the Orthodox Jew, or "The Cross, the Sword, and the Arm of the Lord" (one of several paramilitary, neo-Nazi Pentecostal groups), and other isolated religious groups because the boundaries between the researcher and the researched are clearer, more objective, easier to keep distinct.

By and large, approaches to the study of folk religion in this country have been narrowly confined to descriptions of the more sensational aspects of fundamentalist religions, and to attempts to define "folk religion" or the "folk church."[1] Only a few folklorists have developed ways to analyze specific folk religious genres such as conversion narratives, testimonies, sermons, religious music and song, or healing rituals.[2] The study of folk religion has been shaped largely by anthropological approaches that separate the components of religious behavior into "official" (elite) and "practical" (folk) categories, though often recognizing the interfacing and syncretism of the two, often symbiotic, traditions.[3] John Messenger strongly supports the common distinction between the study of folk religions of peasants and the study of survivals of primitive beliefs among "civilized" folk. In this narrow view, myths and legends form the core of folk belief systems, are unwritten, "inconsistent," and "poorly integrated." Religions of civilized nations, on the other hand, codify "narratives in the scriptures and auxiliary texts and, over time, come to form consistent, logically integrated, closed systems of thought that explain all phenomena of the universe."[4]

Messenger's own work with religion in Ireland led him to conclude that the islanders qualified as folk because the peasants had a stable agricultural economy based on simple technology and barter; they maintained a low standard of living; and they relied on family for support and continuity. Such a view of the folk harkens back to the very beginnings of folklore as a discipline and reveals Messenger's own reliance on early equations of "folk" and "peasant." According to folklorist Don Yoder, it was Robert Redfield's development of the relationship of the "little tradition" (peasants) and the "great tradition" (urban society) that appealed to folklorists and led to distinctions between "folk religion" and "official religion." This view perpetuates the notion of the larger society as "sophisticated culture" and the smaller society as "marginal," and is supported by Edmund Leach's distinction between "philosophical" and "practical" religions as "religion of the intellectual elite" as opposed to "religious principles which guide the behavior of an ordinary churchgoer."[5]

On the other hand, "folk religion" often refers simply to the survival elements that appear within standardized, official religions. Beliefs, customs, and rituals are isolated and scrutinized for their archaic precedents. Ichiro Hori's *Folk Religion in Japan*, for example, presents folk religion as existing in special relationship with the high-cultural forms of Japanese religion: "these [vague magico-religious] beliefs or primitive elements themselves remain unsystematized theoretically and ecclesiastically but in many ways have penetrated and become interrelated with institutionalized religions." In a similar vein, Joshua Tractenberg describes a Jewish belief in magic and superstition as existing outside the domain of the "official" religion: "ideas and practices that never met with the whole-hearted approval of the religious leaders, beliefs in demons and angels, the practices of magic. . . . If we call these 'folk religion' it is because they expressed the common attitude of the people, as against the official attitude of the Synagogue, to the universe."[6] While Tractenberg suggests that these beliefs cannot be excluded from a study of the field of religion, he concludes that they came to be a part of Judaism through "devious routes" and they "stretch the tenets of the faith almost to the breaking point." According to Yoder, representatives of the official religion (the rabbis) wished either to "eradicate some of these practices or transmute their offensive features."

In response to the neglect and negativism toward such "folk beliefs," Dov Noy, noted Jewish scholar and folklorist, prefers to take note of folk performances of religious narratives.[7] Again, however, a distinction between the "official" and "unofficial" parts of the religion justifies for Noy a story's classification as a "folk-religious item" and part of the folk religion of the group under observation. Both Yoder and Noy call for legitimization of the study of folk religion, as well as recognition of folkloric elements in official religion. Both point out that religious studies, focusing as they do on history of the church and theological and liturgical norms, have largely ignored the "practical" religious behaviors. Yoder and Noy are correct in calling for the legitimization of the study of folk religion, but the notion that folk religious beliefs and practices are "held by a tiny minority" overlooks the pervasiveness in all religions of the oral, traditional, informal, and nonstandardized elements.

Drawing our attention away from specific beliefs and toward the believers, folklorist William Clements, working with fundamentalist groups in Arkansas, suggests that there are ten traits of the "folk church" that have nationwide applicability: orientation to the past, scriptural literalism, consciousness of Providence, emphasis on evangelism, informality, emotionalism, moral rigorism, sectarianism, egalitarianism, and relative isolation of church plants.[8] But Clements, too, becomes too concerned with where the church plant is located and whether or not the ministers belong to an organization.

None of these approaches adequately isolates what it is the folklorist ought to focus on in the study of folk religion. Many scholars are merely electing to study folk religious elements of main-line denominations or are overly concerned with identification of what constitutes an idealized "folk church." Too often these studies become item oriented, or focus only on the ways in which some religions are primitive, or off-beat, or are survivals. A more productive avenue of research focuses on religious practices within the context of a particular group, because these are the creative but traditional aspects of the religion. The critical question becomes: what in this religion is *traditional*—that is, what is being passed down from generation to generation, or from group member to member, in an informal, largely oral, manner? Beliefs, behaviors, practices, rituals acquired in such a manner will take on the characteristics of an oral, traditional style. They will be formulaic, stylized, patterned, ritualistic because they *are* oral. Occasionally, in the fundamentalist Pentecostal denomination, we can locate churches in which nearly every element of the religious service is reflective of the oral, traditional style. A "folk church," then, is not a folk church because its members are poor or marginal or psychologically unstable, but because the theological premises on which it stands, the order of the service, the plan of salvation, the practices and rituals performed at each service, are all established, maintained, and performed orally by the collective group involved. These churches do tend to be autonomous. Although the verbal genres characteristic of one church will be observable and recognizable in other churches of the same denomination, the performance style, the order of the service, even the religious language may vary. It is this tension between what is conservative and what is dynamic that makes the religion a folk religion.[9]

The focus of our understanding of folk religion ought not to be on conceptions of who the folk really are and, by extension, what religion they happen to practice. Nor ought we to concern ourselves merely with folk elements within official religions, although the syncretism of the two and the vitality of the folk elements are certainly worthy of examination. Rather, folk religion must be recognized as a traditional religion that thrives in individual, independent religious groups that owe little allegiance to hierarchical powers. Each church shares certain tenets of belief and religious experience with other similar denominational religious groups in the geographic area but develops, from its own traditions, its own order of service, protocol, male/female participation, and group identity. Pentecostals form a distinct folk religious group, recognized as such both by the group and by the rest of the community. They have a shared base of religious beliefs and experiences that is exhibited and transmitted via traditional channels within the religious community. These channels are the various religious practices and verbal genres available to the members of the church congregation and will be the focus of this study.

Our understanding of what is said and done in a small Pentecostal church in southern Indiana in 1980 can be enhanced by recalling the local roots of the religion and examining the roles of men and women who have established, nurtured, and transmitted the tenets and traditions of this largely oral religion. Pentecostalism can be traced back to the camp meeting revivals of the nineteenth century and Methodist conceptions of holiness, but the present-day Pentecostal experience is best understood within its own historical and sociocultural context.

A thread runs through the history of Pentecostalism, and through this study of that religion. It has to do with the participation and the role of women. The focus on women is not an artifical one; to focus on the women and how they speak is to offer a view of the religion not possible from any other vantage point. The study of religion, focused as it often is on theological and liturgical issues, has historically been the study of religious *man*. In his robes and crowns, the flamboyant male struts across the platform and calls attention to himself and denies women an equal role, insisting upon his own closer physical affinity to a male god. In many religions, therefore, the role of the female is denigrated to one of subject, supplicant, singer, and observer. It is not surprising, then, that many female religious expressions lie in the realm of the traditional rather than the official. Women create home altars; they become possessed and speak in tongues; they become witches and midwives. In Pentecostal church services, on the other hand, women testify, preach, and pray. They have developed a forum for religious expression, and they use it to fashion the faith that means so much to them.

My own fieldwork supports the contention that Pentecostalism is largely a "woman's religion," yet I do not accept the notion that women flock to this religion because of their more hysterical or unbalanced nature. Rather, this study seeks to describe how Pentecostals establish themselves as a distinct folk group—through language and codes of behavior, and, significantly, through dress codes for the female members; how women have functioned in the development of the Pentecostal religion; and what role the religion plays in their lives, as well as how the religion controls their lives.

Certainly, the use of verbatim texts has long been at the heart of folklore scholarship, but analysis of verbatim religous genres has not been widespread. Bruce Rosenberg's landmark study, *The Art of the American Folk Preacher,* is nearly twenty years old and has not been followed by anything akin to it in content or scope, although Gerald Davis's recent study, *I Got the Word in Me and I Can Sing It, You Know,* continues the tradition of studying the chanting black male preacher.[10] Jeff Titon has recently published a long verbatim transcript of various religious genres in a booklet written to accompany the issue of a record entitled "Powerhouse of God," but such a publication will have a limited distribution.[11] These approaches have added to our knowledge of religious verbal art, but few, if any, analyze the actual words of the believers as they speak within the religous service. The people in this book are not so much talking about their religion, although I have asked them to do that, too, but rather speaking their religion: this is a study of what people say and do while celebrating their religion. Studies of religious language are not, in fact, the same as studies of religious speech; speakers may or may not use identifiable "religious language," but the fact that a prayer is prayed, a testimony given, a healing enacted, or a sermon preached within the bounded religious service time makes that speech religious.[12] This study attempts, then, to isolate what those religious genres are; to determine which ones operate within a Pentecostal religious service, as well as when and where in respect to one another they coexist; to analyze the performance style of delivery, the poetic form, the content, and the structure of these religious genres; to delineate which genres are available as forums for verbal expression to men or to women and how they are manipulated differently by the sexes; and, finally, to offer a suggestion as to how we might understand the political power of religious speech for the female members of the religiocultural community by examining their spoken testimonies.

Studies of religion tend to focus on the powerful within denominations, usually the male pastors and preachers, because they espouse the eschatological foundations of Christian belief and claim the right to preach and preserve those beliefs. It is these beliefs, though, that are most likely to be reduced to writing, formalized into doctrine, and thus no longer subject to change and modification. But the spontaneously created religious genres spoken aloud by the group members in a Pentecostal religious service are excellent examples of oral tradition in a modern context. While they have a formularized, standard format and appropriate slots for performance within the religious service, they are at the same time available to the speaker-performers as avenues for personal creativity. The precarious balance of the oral-formulaic nature and artistic variability of verbal genres has been examined in this century by Homeric scholars Albert Lord and Milman Parry, in their attempts to understand the *Odyssey* as an orally rendered folk poem, sung for centuries by singers each relying on standard oral formulas, themes, and stanzas but at the same time enjoying the opportunity for creative elaboration.[13] Their respect for the oral tradition and their insight into the stabilizing and artistic aspects of verbal art have aided all folklorists who work with verbatim texts.

Within the context of Christian religion in the United States, Pentecostalism offers creative religion to its members; the denomination has a history of breaking with longstanding Christian beliefs and rituals, of offering an arena for a participatory, charismatic religious experience. Pentecostal churches have developed traditional genres for verbal expression within the format of the religious service. Discourse rules apply to formulaic structures, but manipulation is possible as each traditional singer, pray-er, testifier, healer, or preacher brings to the form her or his own creative impulse. As folk performers, the verbal experts stand and deliver performances that are subject to critical evaluation by the other members of their group; prayers, testimonies, and sermons are all under scrutiny. Inappropriate performances will be scandals; appropriate deliveries will elicit favorable responses from the audience; in fact, audience approval is often signaled by overt audience behavior—dancing, singing, shouting.

Within this religious context, then, it follows that the religion could offer slots for individual expression to various members of the group. I have elected to examine the testimonies of Pentecostal women, in the final chapter of this book, to illustrate how verbal performances are bound to a traditional structure, how they allow for personal creativity, and how they offer to the women performers the possibility for temporary control of the religious service. As an oral religion, Pentecostalism relies on the power of words and the ability of the speakers of those words to release that power.

CHAPTER ONE

The Field Situation

I don't know how you girls feel or whether you realize that or not, but see, you know all about my life and I don't know anything about yours.

LIMESTONE is at the heart of southern Indiana industry. Much of the land south of Bloomington is pockmarked with the unsightly rubble left by the quarry crews. Cavernous abandoned pits left by the bulldozers are filled now with filmy green water; bits and pieces of rusting machinery lie half buried in the piles of dirt and sand. The land will never be restored to its natural beauty. Crude barbed-wire fences serve little purpose but to accentuate an already ugly scene. Of course, other quarries in the region further to the north are actively being mined, but the gutted landscape here tells the story of generations of limestone laborers. This book is not about the laborers, however, or their labors in the limestone quarries. It is, rather, the story of many of their womenfolk and of the religion that predominates in this working-class region.

In 1978 I moved into a rural neighborhood south of Bloomington, near the heart of limestone country. Most of my neighbors' husbands worked the mines or the quarries to the south near Bedford and Heltonville. My first encounters with my women neighbors were at the mailboxes. As in many rural areas, our boxes sat primly side by side, all in a row, sometimes twenty to a plank, at the end of the gravel road. That's where I met Beula Estes.

Mrs. Estes, a large, plump woman with snow-white hair pulled back from her face into a full bun, stood near our mailboxes that morning and stunned me with her life's story at our very first meeting. She told me how tough life is for quarry folk, told me how she had raised her kids by herself, after her first husband died in the mines, until she remarried. She told with tears in her eyes how her very own daughter, whose car surely I'd seen, was suffering an identical fate. This study of Pentecostal quarry folk in southern Indiana began with this early morning mailbox conversation. In time, I learned much more about Beula Estes, her world view, and, ultimately, about her Pentecostal religion.

> My husband was electrocuted, you know, in a quarry accident, been twenty-eight years ago in July. We was getting ready for one of them basket dinners at church, you know, and that morning I'd ataken him to work and then seemed like it weren't more than an hour later, they was there telling me that he was dead. The quarry had been without power, you know, and they couldn't figure out why and he was down there trying to figure out what was the matter and there was a big cable, you know, laying on a wire fence and he put his hand on that fence, you know, and it killed him instantly. They had to close the quarry for two or three days, the men was so shook up over that. There were three deaths right then, all in the space of a few weeks. Two weeks before my husband, a man was crushed to death between two large slabs of stone, just crushed to death. And my husband's best friend Benny was so shook up about my husband's death, he went home and told his wife, said, "I'll be the next one." And she said, "Benny, don't talk like that." But two weeks to the day Benny was standing

> between two railway cars and when they were coupled he got crushed between them. Two weeks to the day. He knew, you see, he could feel that he'd be the next.

Beula learned that I was a newcomer to this area, that I knew only of the sand and the cotton in Missouri's bootheel. She told me why quarry life was so difficult, explaining that the rock can only be worked in the warmth of the summer months. The rock has to be wet and then let dry in the sun. In the winter, she said, it gets hard and will break if you try to cut it out. So, in the winter, they all were forced to live on compensation and it was never enough. Quarry life was a tough life, she said more than once. All her life she had scrubbed the clothes of her father, of her brothers, of her husbands when they returned from the quarries. "I remember what my daddy and my first husband, and even Marvin, when we was first married, that was twenty-three years ago, would look like when they first got home. What a mess they'd be. You know, there's clean dirt and dirty dirt and this was the dirtiest dirt ever and we didn't have no washing machine only a scrub board and them clothes seemed like they'd never come clean."

When Beula's first husband died, they already had six children and they had recently taken in a niece and a nephew, whose parents had been killed. "It was real hard on me when my husband died. Someone else took the boy, you know, to lighten my load. But the girl stayed with us and she knows her history all right but she calls me Mom just like my own kids. But I had all them kids alone for nearly five years." Then Beula married Marvin. For a time Marvin also worked in the quarries as had his father and brothers before him. But Beula was relieved when he found work for the lumber company and worked there for years. "But my daddy, my daddy worked in the quarry since he was a strip of a boy, just a strip of a boy. He used to carry

water. That's how they all started then. Now, it seems a lot of the young folks have a choice and not so many want to go into quarry work cause it's a rough, dirty, dangerous business."

But Beula knows that many of the young men in this area still turn to the quarries to make a living, especially those boys who do not finish high school and who marry young and start families. Her daughter's husband worked in a local quarry and had been killed only a few months before. Now, the girl is forced to support her three children, and she never finished high school either. Beula does a lot of babysitting for her daughter; she is glad to see her daughter and her children almost daily now. She enjoys being able to help take responsibility for her daughter's family. But it saddens her to see her daughter suffer the same fate that she had.

> You know, after my husband got killed, we had a little white dog, and after my husband got killed that little dog would go to the end of the lane just like he done every day and sit and wait, at exactly the time when he would have come home, and then he'd begin to howl and that dog would howl and he'd howl when he knowed he wasn't coming home. And the only way I could make him shut up was to bring him into the house and then alst he'd do was sit in front of the back door and whine. So, now when I hear a dog howl it kindly bothers me on account of that little old white dog we had nearly thirty years ago.

Beula Estes knew right away she'd found a good listener, and Beula loved to talk. Soon she and I were spending long mornings over coffee as she told me of her life, her family, her hardships. She would drag out volumes and volumes of scrapbooks and albums to show me a pasted up, frag-

mented collage of her life. During my months of friendship with Beula, I learned of the cultural world to which she belonged. I recognized a traditional, even Puritan view, which syncretized notions of witches and devils with the Holy Ghost and a personalized Christ figure. Everything that happened in Beula's world had something to do with God's will or with Satan's wily intervention in her life, and, for me at least, it was largely indistinguishable which force was at work. If she lost something, it was the work of Satan; when she found it, it was because God showed her where it was. If difficulties became more than she thought she could bear, it was Satan tempting her and God testing her faith at the same time. If people died or suffered illness and misfortune, it was God's will.

> I want to show you a piece out of Sunday's paper. This is about a witch named Aileen Davis. Now I knew her and she *was* a witch. She lived just down the road from me and we all knowed she was a witch. Oh, yes, and we believed in them, too. Well, you know they are scripture. The Bible talks about witchery. They've got a contract with the devil, you know. My daddy used to tell us about witches. Back then, though, you knew who was witches and you knowed what they did. I remember once during thrashing, the thrashers would help each other, twenty or thirty of them at one farm, and the women would gather and cook a big meal, spread big tables. When the men came in that day they said, "Well, the horse has been bewitched." They knew who it was, too. A woman had been there to borrow something. "Don't let her have anything," the men said. She had a teacup, wanted to borrow some sugar. But the women turned her down. She came three times, see. "Don't let her have it," they said,

> "and it will break the spell." Well, that made her mad. She'd made that horse sick, see, but then the horse got well.

Beula told me many stories about witches, most of them traditional narratives, or stories replete with traditional motifs. Many of her stories associated witches with the dairy, a long-standing association. She told of a milkmaid her grandfather told about who could milk the fringe on a hand towel, "milk a full bucket of pure white milk." But when she did, the cow would get sick. So they fired her and told her to go far away, because they knew the cow would die. She recalled her mother telling her and her sisters how girls would become witches—that they would pray and pray to the devil until they were completely controlled by him. Her mother told her of a girlfriend of hers who had once visited a known witch who told her to "pray to the devil until it's black as night." Her friend did, and all kinds of demons appeared, the air was full of them. Her friend was terrified and cried out, "Oh, Lord, help me," and the air cleared immediately and she never missed church again in her life. Beula figured people wanted to become witches because they can cause things to happen, because they feel powerful. "At night around the fire my daddy used to tell us about witches, used to scare me to death, but that's what he wanted, wanted us to be afraid so that we would go to church and only trust in Jesus not to pray to the devil *ever*. He never told us any fairy stories. He would never tell anything untrue; he'd only tell us true stories."

At first this strange juxtaposition of devils and witches with strict religious inclinations baffled me, but in time I have come to understand more about this fundamentalist religion that recognizes a close association between the natural and the supernatural worlds. In fact, the most fundamental tenet of this Christian faith requires a mandatory experience of spirit possession by the Holy Ghost, accompanied by speaking in unknown tongues. Daily exposure to this realm of paranormal religious experience and a blanket rejection of all things of "this world" provide easy access to and acceptance of nonworldly experiences.

My visits with Beula Estes would always end with her trying to "witness" to me about her Pentecostal religion. She would tell me how good it is to go to church, how much better I'd feel if I would just go, how important religion is in her life. She'd be "right proud," she'd say, to take me to church with her. "I wish you'd come and go to church with us tonight. We're having what my mama used to call a protracted meeting, what they used to call a revival. But we're having this revival for three weeks. It's already been going for five nights and we've been having some powerful preaching and people getting real happy. I go every night. Wouldn't miss it for the world. Maybe Miss Sutton would like to go, too."

Irene Sutton, our neighbor, was Pentecostal, too, but usually does not attend the same church as Beula Estes. A few years ago a group from Beula's congregation broke away and formed their own church congregation. They meet now in an abandoned building on Quarry Rock Lane, not more than three miles from the original church. This is typical in this region. Many of the back roads have several small Baptist and Pentecostal churches, most with small congregations—split on a minor theological point or a personality conflict. But during the revivals and camp meetings, nearly everyone in the area will attend the "protracted meetings."

Later that same week, I crossed the dirt road that led up a small hill to a rickety old house where "Miss" Irene Sutton lives. I found her huddled in the kitchen drinking tea from an old cracked cup, a thick white one like you get in country restaurants. She was dressed in a thin and faded cotton dress with men's work boots and socks and what appeared to be several jackets and a woolen scarf, very worn. The room was cold, heated only by a small electric heater in the corner. Quilts and comforters were hanging over all the doorways leading in four directions from the kitchen. The light was poor as the day was gray and overcast. Irene Sutton is a widow. Her husband and father both worked in the quarries around Bedford for years. Her husband then opened the only sawmill in the area. They had ten children. He was killed at the mill when the youngest was seven years old. Several of her "boys" still live close by and stop at her house daily to check on her and to see if she needs anything. She told me she didn't know very much first-hand about the quarries. She just knew that quarry life was a tough life. Only once, she said, had she ever even gone to see the working quarry. She and another girl went to the quarry where their husbands worked and watched from the hill. She said she "just wanted to look at it."

> What I knew about it was pretty much based on what my husband said when he got home, which wasn't much as my husband didn't talk much. I do recall him telling me about how my niece's husband got killed down there. He was smashed when a derrick hook holding a huge rock came down and killed him. The pity of it was he had two little kids, two little girls. My niece had to raise them by herself. I remember, too, when they found that woman who worked at the creamery floating around in the water that had collected, you know, in the quarry.

Already the stories seemed familiar. So many husbands and fathers maimed or killed; so many wives and mothers left alone to provide for the children. I was not prepared to hear stories that sounded so much like the stories we have come to expect from the mining areas in Appalachia, in

Kentucky and Tennessee. These quarry women were survivors and they were not sentimental about it. Collectively they began to tell the same story.

> I remember trying to get the grease and the dirt out of my daddy's clothes, and my husband's, too. Used to put lard on it to get that dirt out. It was nasty work. Made my husband deaf, too, couldn't hear a thing I don't think. There was so much noise. He used to work on the machine siding, you know, which was so loud that it made him deaf. Lots of them go deaf. My Uncle Pete got killed in the quarry, not too long ago, must have been twenty, thirty, no maybe thirty-five years ago. There was another guy, too, who went to school with me who got killed in that same quarry. But he was a young man, not married. I can't hardly remember getting married, hah, just kindly got married to change my name, I guess.

As she talked, Irene began to fumble through drawers and shoe boxes gathering together what seemed to be millions of tiny pieces of bright fabric. "I'm fixing to piece a quilt, got all the pieces laid out in here on the bed. Would you like to see it? I'll show you a comfort I've got, too, that's sixty-five years old. My mother made it." Our quilt piece arranging was interruped by the visit of one of Irene's sons, who had brought her a sack of drugs from the town pharmacy. She told him that he could just take them all back to town because she wasn't about to use any of them. She showed me, and him, what she preferred to use: garlic tablets and ginseng. She pulled away her scarf to reveal a pungent poultice she had mixed that morning for her sore throat: turpentine, coal oil, and lard. She spoke of "mullen tea" and told me to drink catnip tea for stomach problems.

Like Beula's, Irene's world is a traditional one of home

remedies and quilt-making. In 1978 she did not have, nor did she desire, a television set. Her table AM radio was her only link to a world beyond her own—except for church. Irene asked if her son could come back that evening around seven to take her to the protracted meeting they were having down the road. As he and I both left her house, Miss Sutton began energetically to beg me to come go with her to the revival meeting. Her eyes were bright as she told me how wonderful these meetings had been and about how much they meant to her. She *loved* going to church, she told me, it's what she looked forward to each day.

Fifteen miles down the road from Irene Sutton's is Johnson's Creek Church, the Pentecostal church featured in this book. Half a mile further, on the blacktop, is the home of Alice Benson. She lives in a modest home set back from the road with her three youngest children and her husband, Albert, who works in a quarry near Bedford. Alice's father is a Pentecostal preacher. She has gone to Pentecostal services all her life and thinks of herself first as a Pentecostal woman. Albert is not "saved" and refuses to go to church with her. This is, perhaps, the saddest part of Alice's life and has brought her years of anguish. Her parents warned her when she was an impressionable young girl of fifteen that Albert Benson was not the type ever to go to church. He worked and played too hard. He liked the bars too much. They were right. Albert has never listened to Alice's pleading to join the church. She is just thankful that he does not prevent her from going to church herself and from taking the boys. She knows there will come a day when the boys will no longer go with her and when they will join their dad. "My husband works at Bedford at Engle Stone Company. He's worked in stone for years and years. He worked at Bloomington for a long time. Seemed like, maybe fourteen or fifteen years, he worked there, then it shut down. Only other jobs he's had been working on the roads in Monroe County. But stone mills don't shut down as much as the actual quarries. He's a planerman, now, he cuts." Alice talks, too, about quarry life. She still has to scrub her husband's grimy clothes, and in the winter she has to feed a family of five solely on what she has put by through the summer months. But Alice would rather talk about her religion, because it is her religion that keeps her going, that gives her joy in an otherwise depressing life. Her best memories were of large groups of family members going to church together. She recalls how one preacher got an automobile and would go around gathering up all the neighbors on Dutch Ridge Road.

> When *I* was a kid, well, I remember we went to church a lot. And when we wasn't in school or church, we'd play church and my aunt that stayed with us, she'd get the guitar. She couldn't play it, but she'd play it, you know. She'd play church songs and we would sing. Back then they had prayer meetings in homes and they'd go to a different home every night. And I can remember Mom and Dad would just take the furniture out of the living room and they'd put just boards, on rocks or stumps, sticks of wood was what it was. And course the old house was pretty flimsy and Dad would get under it and brace it until the floor wouldn't give. Oh, we'd have a house full.

Alice especially enjoyed recalling the times when people would "get happy" at the various church gatherings—from prayer meetings to camp meetings and revivals. That's why, she said, her dad had to brace up the floor, because folks would get to dancing and stomping around so.

> And I know one time a lady got happy with her accordion and she just shouted all over the house

> with her accordion. What makes me remember that—one of the brothers was telling about it later and called it a piano. One night after that he got up and he testified about seeing this sister shout all over that house with a piano around her neck [laughs heartily]. He meant an accordion, you know. I mean that's just some of the kinds of memories that I have, mostly of being surrounded by lovely Christian people happy in the Lord. They'd do that maybe once a week. I mean we went to different houses and maybe it wasn't once a week, but I know ever so often it would come back home. Everybody would come to our house then and then the next time we'd go somewhere else. And there were so many people I knew that way, you know, all through church. In fact, some of the people that I go to church up here with, you know, I'd know them or their parents from those meetings in people's houses.

Alice can recall when the first Pentecostal preacher came to her church and preached a "Pennycost" message, sometime in the late twenties or early thirties. The man who came with this new religious message, Brother Goddard, stayed in the region for some time trying to convert people to this new religious experience and rebaptizing people "in the name of Jesus." Many of the rural churches changed during this time to Pentecostal assemblies of one kind or another. Alice and her entire family were eventually baptized into this new religion following several weeks of protracted meetings in a camp-meeting tabernacle that still stands not far from Alice's house. "It was just like an open barn. It was just a big building with a roof on it and it had some sides, but the windows were just cut out. And they had meetings in it and it had a sawdust floor. We called it Handy. . . . The old building is in a field kind of growed up, with lots of trees. That's about all they ever used it for. The services in there were real old-fashioned. They had guitar music and people sang and if they felt like they wanted to get up and walk or shout or whatever they felt like the Lord wanted them to do, they did it."

Alice does not live very far from Johnson's Creek Church and she attends every service she possibly can. She does not drive well and her husband is reluctant to let her drive any farther than to the church and back. He makes her promise that she will begin her trip home immediately after the close of the service. Most of her neighbors are women who attend the same church and who have grown up in this same area. Many of their husbands join Alice's during the hours their wives are attending church. Alice recognizes that her life has been constricted. Our visits to her home to talk to her about her life and about her religion obviously became the high points in her weeks.

> It's real hard to make friends out here. We live so far from anything and it's mostly church folks that I ever get to see. I had one friend, one friend that wasn't in the church. She lived over the hill, right over here past our horse field. Lived all by herself, she did, with her kids. And folks weren't real friendly to her or nothing, cause she didn't go to church and nobody knew who her husband was or if she was married. Made them kindly nervous about her, I guess. But, sometimes, when there wasn't nobody here I'd kind of sneak across the field and go up there to visit her. And we'd just sit kind of quiet like on her front steps and talk. And I really enjoyed that. I knew it was wrong, but I really liked having her as a friend. But then my husband found out about it and he really told me to stop going up there. So, I did. And, see, like I don't know how you girls feel or

> whether you realize it or not, but see, you know all about my life but I don't know a thing about yours.

When we asked Alice about her church, about what her religion meant to her, it was as though she could never make us understand just how critical it was to her life, to her survival.

> Church is just something, it gives me something to live on, see? I don't know of anything else that I could get to fulfill my life, fill that spot that—I mean, I don't *do* anything else. I don't know what I'd do, if something would happen to this little church up here, I don't know where I'd go or what I'd do, really. I would just hate awful bad for something to happen and our little church, you know, go down. You just begin to love these people. Just like they're part of your family. There's a real closeness there. Like two "sisters" in the church can be just as close as two sisters. People in Pentecost churches don't go out and find entertainment outside, they find it in the church.

The world of Beula Estes, Irene Sutton, and Alice Benson is a traditional one. They have grown up with the oral, traditional stories and religion of their families and of this southern Indiana region. They trust their illnesses to the natural herbs and poultices their mothers and grandmothers taught them—and to God. They hold tight to a strong belief in the supernatural world. Beula believes in ghosts because members of her family still relate to her their own late-night supernormal experiences in the bogs and deep woods near Brown County. She knows there are witches because when a cow gets sick or dies it is because a strange neighbor woman has spelled it. Belief in both witches and herb medicines is possible because of a strong belief in Satan as a living reality, a daily and constant threat to health and well-being. Almost all of them have grown up near the quarries. Quarry work has fed their mothers' families, their own families, and continues to feed many of their daughters' and sons' families. Often, their stories are uncannily similar; the daughters' lives seem but a mirror image of the mothers'. Waiting out the long winters when there is no work, raising children alone with no father in the home, finding work and learning to cope become the main components of their lives.

Beula, Irene and Alice are all Pentecostal women. Their faith demands that each one have a personal encounter with the Holy Spirit. This encounter with a supernatural spirit will be manifested by a public exhibition of tongue-speaking. They are at ease with dancing in the church, swooning "in the spirit," and watching their sisters "fall out" onto the floor in a trance. For them, the supernormal, the supernatural and the normal worlds cross often. Church is not a Sunday-only obligation; it is often a seven-night-a-week ecstatic experience. The tongue-speaking, the trances, the shouting are all put into perspective during the service through the communicative mode of the testimonies. Here, the members tell of their experiences, interpret them, and in so doing, guide their brother and sister members toward a greater understanding of their own experiences and of the world in which they live.

Pentecostalism, as a new religious denomination, did not emerge overnight. The various components recognized today as standard Pentecostal attributes—such as trance and charismatic behaviors, tongue-speaking, and shouting in the spirit—developed piecemeal over nearly a hundred years. The enthusiastic worshipping style that characterizes Pentecostal church services today is reminiscent of early nineteenth-century Methodist revivals and camp meetings.[1] The strict fundamentalist taboos and regulations imposed upon Pentecostal believers stem largely from the strong "Holiness" tradition, which was itself an outgrowth of John Wesley's Methodist notions of sanctification.[2] But the belief that salvation and sanctification could be had in a single experience of possession by the Holy Ghost and tongue-speaking is uniquely Pentecostal; it combined ideas that had prevailed in Christian tradition for decades.

Methodism and the Holiness movement preceded Pentecostalism historically and anticipated its doctrines; both, of course, continue to exist as religious movements today. Among these overlapping histories it is difficult to pinpoint a definite time and place for the birth of the Pentecostal denomination. Much of the confusion arises from the indiscriminate use of the words "Pentecostal" and "Holiness" by lay people and scholars, as well as the striking number of churches that are Pentecostal but whose names may not so indicate.[3] Confusion also arises because "Pentecostal" is often linked merely with emotional church behavior or, more often, with tongue-speaking.

It is important to note that the Pentecostal movement in the United States and the religion that came to be recognized as Pentecostalism began when the experience of tongue-speaking was accepted as evidence of the presence of the Holy Ghost, and when a small group of believers began to equate salvation with just such an experience of tongue-speaking. The entire story of the development of the Pentecostal movement and the various Assemblies of God that emerged from roots in Methodism and the Holiness movement need not be recounted here. The following discussion is presented primarily to aid in understanding the Pentecostals with whom this study is concerned and to chart their pilgrimage to southern Indiana.

John Wesley's eighteenth-century conception of Methodism caught on in the United States and has been one of the strongest religious traditions in this country. Wesley preached salvation by the "first blessing," which was instant sanctification, or perfection attainable in this life. A sanctified believer, according to Wesley, could achieve "perfect love toward God and man." The eighty-one-page manifesto, *A Plain Account of Christian Perfection as Believed and Taught by the Rev. Mr. John Wesley*, issued in 1739, served Methodist and perfectionist groups for two centuries. Early Methodism was largely a reaction against the extreme Calvinism that had dominated English social, religious, and political life during the seventeenth century. According to Vinson Synan, a scholar and a believer, the "creedal rigidity, liturgical strictness, and ironclad institutionalism that had depersonalized religion had rendered it incapable of serving the needs of the individual believer."[4] Methodism allowed any man, woman, or child the saving experience, rejecting the notion of the elected few. Methodists sought the personal experiences of conversion and sanctification. According to John Nichol, another believer, "sanctification or the 'second blessing' was seen as an experience subsequent and distinct from justification or conversion. Its effect is the eradication of natural depravity or inbred sin."[5]

As often happens in religious movements as they become more official and standardized, some of Wesley's followers came to find his Methodism staid and restricting. Eventually, many of his followers thought Wesley's leadership had lost sight of the importance of the search for sanctification or holiness. Thus, the Holiness movement was born, composed primarily of disenchanted Methodists. In an effort to restore some of the enthusiasm of early Methodism, leaders of the schism called the first "National Camp Meeting Association for the promotion of Christian Holiness" and urged anyone sympathetic toward the search for "holiness" to attend, regardless of denominational ties. "Come, brothers and sisters of the various denominations, and let us, in this forest meeting, as in other meetings for the promotion of holiness, furnish an illustration of evangelical union, and make common supplication for the descent of the Spirit upon ourselves, the church, the nation, and the world."[6] Intended for the sole purpose of seeking the state of holiness, this camp meeting was held in Vineland, New Jersey, on July 17, 1867. This was just the beginning; Vineland was an unqualified success, and its fame spread quickly. Holiness camp meetings sprang up all over the country.

Camp meetings were largely characterized by what appeared to outsiders as wild evangelizing and came to be referred to as representative of the "old-time religion." The instigators of this break with Methodism claimed that the Holiness movement adhered more closely to the basic tenets of Methodism than did Methodism itself, especially in its rigid compliance with doctrines of Christian perfection. Wesley's strict admonitions against all alcoholic drinking, dancing, theater-going, card-playing, and swearing, and his restrictions on women's dress were embraced fully and further elaborated by Holiness groups to prohibit, in time, Coca-Cola, chewing gum, rings, bracelets, earbobs, and neckties. The emphasis of the Holiness doctrine, which would later serve as the core of Pentecostalism, included the seeking of a blessing, which ought to be received subsequent to and distinct from conversion; a submission to the Spirit in all affairs of life; a lifetime effort to win converts and rejuvenate the spiritual lives of the faithful; a vibrant hope in the imminent return of Christ; and abandonment of the world and all manifestations of "worldliness."

In time, the rural South and the Middle West emerged as the predominant areas of the Holiness movement, embracing the doctrines wholeheartedly. Traveling evangelists brought the Holiness message to the most isolated communities in these regions, and here the message took root. These preachers laid great emphasis on dress and denial of "worldly amusements," as well as on denunciations of the coldness and formality of the Methodist church. In an attempt to understand why Holiness caught on in the rural South and Midwest, some scholars have suggested that rather than trying to reform society, which they knew they could not do, rural folk rejected it. Within Holiness the greatest "social sins" were not poverty, inequality, or unequal distribution of the wealth, but rather the effects of the theater, ball games, dancing, lipstick, cigarettes, and liquor. The appeal of Holiness was inherent in the optimistic promise of attainable perfection for everyone. The Holiness Movement emphasized the warmth, feeling, emotional religious experience, and morality that began in Methodism and soon came to be known as "heart religion."

The two largest Holiness denominations that resulted from the national Holiness movement were the Church of the Nazarene and the Pilgrim Holiness Church. Although many early Nazarene churches included the word "pentecostal" in their names, they later dropped that word to publicly disassociate themselves from the Pentecostal movement of the 1900s, when they concluded that emotionalism and tongue-speaking had become more important in that movement than sanctification. The Pilgrim Holiness group was the forerunner of modern-day Pentecostalism, and the most important church in this regard was one that emerged in Iowa around 1894, called the "Fire-Baptized Holiness Church." Its leader, John Fletcher, previously a Baptist minister who had been sanctified, began to call for a "third blessing" (to complement the first blessing of conversion and the second blessing of sanctification), which he called "the baptism of the Holy Ghost and fire" or simply "The Fire." His revivals in the Midwest gave rise once again to the emotional fervor of the early Methodist revivals; those receiving the fire would "shout, scream, speak in tongues, fall into trances, and even get the jerks." Fletcher's new interpretation caused much concern and frequent rejection by many within the Holiness movement because the Holiness advocates had always associated the second blessing, of sanctification (holiness) with a baptism by the Holy Ghost and considered both to be aspects of the same experience. Note that no connection was being made at this time between the baptism of the Holy Ghost and speaking in tongues. Both were occurring in the camp meetings; the baptism of the Holy Ghost was sought, and some people who "got into the spirit" often spoke in tongues, but there was no hint that this baptism and/or tongue-speaking were necessary prerequisites to salvation. The most radical of the preachers of this fire-baptized movement became more and more obsessed with the notion of repeated emotional experiences; the meetings became prolonged as members sought for yet another ecstatic encounter. Eventually, preachers were calling for not only a third blessing, but a fourth, a fifth, and even a sixth. One preacher praised God for the blood that cleans up, the Holy Ghost that fills up, the fire that burns up, and the dynamite that blows up![7]

By the late 1890s, several Holiness preachers had experienced tongue-speaking in Holiness churches and camp meetings and were beginning to search for this ecstatic third blessing. The early practice of tongue-speaking in American religious contexts received a great deal of attention, not all of it sympathetic. Revivals in Tennessee, where "praying through" was often accompanied by tongue-speaking, caused great excitement, and many nonbelievers blasted the tongue-speakers as practicing "heresy." As more people experienced "the tongues" (including children), opposition became serious. Perhaps the opposition served to fire the spirit of the believers.

Although tongue-speaking among Holiness believers had occurred long before 1900, it was not linked to salvation until a group of religious students at Bethel College in Topeka, Kansas, found evidence for the connection in their Bibles. Directed by their teacher, Charles F. Parham, to seek the answer to the question, "What is the Bible evidence of the Baptism of the Holy Ghost?" this group of thirty to forty women and men sought the answer for days. Using only their Bibles as a guide, the students came up with the answer that the evidence of the Holy Ghost was speaking in tongues.[8] The scriptural basis for their answer comes largely from the Book of Acts, although there are other biblical references that link tongue-speaking with the infilling of the Holy Ghost. The primary scripture that convinced them was Acts 2:1-4, which describes the descent of the Holy Ghost upon 120 believers who were in the Upper Room praying and fasting: "And when the day of Pentecost was fully come, they were all with one accord in one place, And suddenly there came a sound from heaven as of a rushing mighty wind, and it filled all the house where they were sitting. And there appeared unto them cloven tongues like as of fire, and it sat upon each of them. And they were all filled with the Holy Ghost, and began to speak with other tongues, as the Spirit gave them utterance." Parham's students sought to replicate this experience. In time, several of the students did receive the baptism and spoke in tongues; then the group received the baptism en masse. Practicing Pentecostals claim this as the birth of Pentecostalism because it most closely parallels the outpouring of the Holy Spirit in the biblical Upper Room as described in the New Testament. This is the account they give for the adoption of the name "Pentecosts" as well, because the biblical episode occurred during Pentecost.

From Kansas the Pentecostal message spread all over the country. The single most important doctrinal issue that distinguished it from the Holiness movement was the belief that speaking in tongues was the evidence of the possession of the Holy Ghost and that this experience was as necessary for salvation as conversion and sanctification. Although tongue-speaking had occurred time and again in revivals and camp meetings, it had never before become the center of attention. With Pentecostalism came a unified effort to seek and experience this proof of the Holy Ghost in the converted.

Pentecostal preachers began to preach what they called the

"full gospel," a term still used today to identify a legitimate Pentecostal group. The full gospel is a combination of old doctrines and new emphases: the biblical emphasis on salvation and justification by faith; the stress on divine healing; the doctrine of the premillennial return of Christ; belief in a Holy Spirit whose baptism empowers a Christian to live victoriously and to witness effectively and enables the believer to perform the supernatural.[9] According to Nichol, the Pentecostals were "almost rabid in their assertion that glossolalia always accompany an 'infilling of the Holy Ghost.' "[10]

Between 1901 and 1906, the fervor for the "Pentecostal experience" centered largely in Houston, Texas, where Charles Parham and other leaders had congregated to spread the message. By 1906, the Pentecostal movement took root in Los Angeles, where outpourings of the "Latter Rain," or "The Fire," occurred with regularity in meetings in Bonnie Brae Street, and then for three years was manifested in the now-famous church on Azusa Street.[11] Although the location of the church in a poor black community created a standard stereotype that the movement was predominantly embraced by black Christians, the church on Azusa Street, as well as others that sprang up during these formative years, drew its congregation from both the black and the white communities. Once the press noticed all the noise over on Azusa Street, their negative and somewhat derisive illustrated accounts often served as advertisement and swelled the crowds even more. Block-Hoell notes that it was in the Seattle papers that the Pentecostals were first referred to as "Holy Rollers" and that their Methodist forerunners had been referred to as "Holy Jumpers." He also notes that non-Pentecostals referred to the movement as the "Tongues Movement." By September, 1906, the Pentecostal movement claims to have had 13,000 followers in the United States and by the end of the year Pentecostalism had reached Europe and Asia.[12]

Again, preachers traveled the countryside preaching the Pentecostal message in Baptist and Methodist churches.

Often, one segment of the congregation would respond favorably to this new message and split off from the denominational church to form a separate group and call themselves "Pentecosts" or "Pennycosts." From the beginning, Pentecostals have been inclined to refer to this new faith as the "Pentecostal experience," rejecting such labels as Pentecostal religion, church, or denomination. In a fairly short time, minute differences about doctrine began to plague the new Pentecostals. Black Pentecostals formed their own official church, the Church of God (Cleveland, Tennessee); white Pentecostals called for a "General Council of the Assemblies of God" in 1914 to formalize the doctrine that conversion and sanctification could be experienced at the same time and managed to alienate Holiness Pentecostals for good. Although Pentecostals talk about the "holiness" aspects of their religion, a clear distinction developed between Holiness sects and Pentecostal sects.

Another even more radical idea split the Pentecostals into two main camps—the trinitarian and the Jesus Only or Oneness Pentecostals. In 1913, at a Pentecostal camp meeting in Los Angeles, evangelist R.E. McAlister declared from the pulpit that the biblical apostles only baptized their converts once in the name of "Jesus" and that the words "Father, Son and Holy Ghost were never used in early Christian baptism."[13] According to Synan, "unknowingly, Evangelist McCalister had fired a shot that would resound throughout the Movement for a year."

The idea caught on in some quarters. Adherents to this new doctrine were rebaptised in Jesus' name and an effort was made to convince and rebaptize the entire Pentecostal movement. But the response was not unanimously positive. The General Council of the Assemblies of God became alarmed by this development and at the meeting in October, 1916, denounced the "Oneness" sects as heretical and established the Assemblies of God as a trinitarian body. While the unitarian point of view is unacceptable to many Pentecostals, it still attracts large numbers of believers. The largest recognized unitarian Pentecostal denomination in the United States today is the United Pentecostal Church, which was created by the merger of several independent unitarian Pentecostal groups. There are, however, literally thousands of Oneness Pentecostal churches in the Midwest that have no affiliation with any major, recognized organization. Contrary to the notion that Jesus Only or Oneness Pentecostals constitute an insignificant proportion of the Pentecostal population, in southern Indiana there are nearly three Oneness churches for every Pentecostal trinitarian church. Oneness believers are staunch about their "Jesus Only" views but are understandably cautious about flaunting their peculiar beliefs. For Oneness Pentecostals to assert that Jesus *is* God strikes many other Christians as heretical and blasphemous. Many Oneness Pentecostals in southern Indiana relate stories of ostracism and persecution arising from their antitrinitarian beliefs.

Rather than being a religion based on official tenets determined by knowledgeable officials, Pentecostalism is based on things that happen to people. And the essence of the experiences, as well as their interpretation, must be communicated to the other members of the group. It is on that foundation that all doctrine rests. Pentecostalism is an oral religion. All members learn to speak a special religious language. It is within the context of the church service that the tenets of the faith are conveyed, interpreted, and stabilized. Stories passed down from grandparents about the early days of traveling preachers who brought the Pentecostal message lay a firm historical foundation for the beliefs of the modern church. A testimony about how someone received the Holy Ghost and spoke in tongues proves to the listeners that this experience can happen and elaborates a model for their own conversion experience.

The Oneness Pentecostals of this study are a tightly knit group of believers who live in a small rural community and depend largely upon one another for their spiritual and social existence. Their radical beliefs set them apart and define their existence as a group. What they believe about their faith and themselves is conveyed by their lifestyles and by what they say when they are together in their community and in their homes, as well as what they say in the context of their church services.

CHAPTER TWO

Maintaining Boundaries

We go into restaurants and people want to know what kind of religion we are, not because what we look like but because they feel a joy about us.

PENTECOSTALS are acutely aware of the many stereotypes, fears, and apprehensions that non-Pentecostals share about them. They realize that most nonbelievers find their beliefs and religious behavior strange at best and abhorrent and primitive at worst. Strong anti-Pentecostal sentiment from outsiders only feeds the fire of Pentecostalism, however, and is proof enough for them that they are a special religious group.[1] The differences between Pentecostals and non-Pentecostals become exaggerated as the in-group strives to establish an identity that distinguishes it from other groups.[2] In general, their conscious withdrawal from the world, their vehement rejection of it, and their refusal to participate in it establishes an effective boundary between "them" and "us." As Max Weber indicates, it is, then, an easy step to making rejection of the world the sure path to salvation.[3] This gives the group the added benefit of believing that they are not only special but are the ones likely to be "saved," while the rest of mankind, happily participating in the world, will eventually suffer an eternity in hell. The various religious behaviors exhibited by Pentecostals are further proof of their specialness and help to stabilize their group identification.[4]

Ethnicity scholars recognize that in many respects religious communities are similar to ethnic groups. Particularly in the case of Pentecostals, where language, dress, behavior, and ethics mark them as distinctly different from other groups adjacent to them in the society as a whole, it is helpful to recognize the importance of boundary establishment and maintenance for the perpetuation of group identity.

Pentecostals are aware of the stereotype that all Pentecostals are poor, uneducated, and drawn to a charismatic religion because they have nothing better. This stereotype, as it exists in southern Indiana, is based largely on the way Pentecostals dress. Most of the communities in this area are typical midwestern farming communities. Pentecostals look different from others in the community because of the dress codes they have adopted. Pentecostal women always wear dresses, and the dresses they wear are usually of somber colors, fall well below the knees, and have long sleeves and high necklines. Outside the home, Pentecostal women are most likely to wear shoes with heels and nylon stockings. Especially in the hot summer months, Pentecostal dress is easily recognizable. Pentecostal women wear no jewelry or makeup and, because they are not allowed to cut their hair, it either falls down their backs or is piled high on their heads in a 1950-ish "beehive" hairstyle or pulled back in a severe bun. It is evident that modern fashion does not dictate what Pentecostal women wear or what they look like. Similarly, Pentecostal men will have shorter haircuts than other men in the community and will be clean-shaven; it is not uncommon for Pentecostal men to sport a "burr" or "flat-top" haircut. Their clothing, too, is recognizable, as they are most likely to "go to town" in black pants, a white shirt, white socks and black shoes. Even Pentecostal young men are not likely to wear blue jeans for fashion, although they may actually work in them.

From the outsider's point of view, the Pentecostal manner of dressing is a mark of the lower class. Pentecostals are associated with poor people everywhere who wear old or plain clothes out of necessity and who do not sport fashionable hairdos because of a lack of opportunity or sophistication. But for the adherents of Pentecostalism, dress embodies an entire complex of notions about "holiness" and displays what a Pentecostal man or woman represents to the rest of the world and to fellow Pentecostals.

Being a model for others to see, attaining perfection in this life, and extolling "holiness" were the attributes sought by those involved in the nineteenth-century Holiness movement. The first edicts John Wesley outlined as necessary for sanctification were adopted and elaborated by the Holiness leaders. The strict doctrines of Christian Holiness specifically forbade drinking, dancing, theater-going, card-playing, and swearing, and outlined restrictions on the dress of believers, especially the women. The term *holiness* as employed by modern Pentecostals still embodies many of the attitudes embraced by the early Holiness movement. One Pentecostal woman defined what holiness means to her: "And the holiness thing. . . . I don't ever want to offend my brother. . . . I don't ever want to offend anyone. I feel like if my dress sleeves are here [motions to elbow] and it would offend my brother, I would put them down to here [motions to wrist]. That's basically how I feel about it."

Pentecostal dress is also a statement to other Pentecostals that the believer is willing to sacrifice all notions of fashion for notions of holiness. Long sleeves and a high neckline signal to Pentecostals a woman's knowledge of the Pentecostal doctrines and her sincere effort to abide by them. In this sense, dress acts as a cohesive bond between Pentecostal women. They can recognize other Pentecostal believers in a grocery or a restaurant. But dress also serves as a comment on the immoral attitudes and styles of the rest of the community. Long skirts and sleeves and high necklines accentuate the short skirts and shorts on the public streets, the braless girls, the daring necklines. Denying the fashions that focus on the female body, and electing, instead, to make a comment for the Lord is seen as the most admirable sacrifice. Non-Pentecostals are not blind to the comments Pentecostals make about the life style of the rest of the world. Not surprisingly, they are often offended and become self-conscious about their own dress and behavior. This is, of course, one intention of the Pentecostals—to draw attention to the dress of others through their own. Their message can be most effective. It is difficult to flaunt immodesty in front of nuns and Pentecostal ladies.

At the same time that Pentecostals are creating distinctive models for members to follow that will differentiate them from others, they are aware that many outsiders consider their behavior extreme: "I think the thing most misunderstood about Pentecost people, they, a lot of people, look at them like they are maybe a freak and that they are completely different from other people 'in the world.' And because of our standards that are set up, the Bible tells us we should be a modest and moderate people and we set up a standard that might seem extreme to the outside world when actually we feel that it's a moderation in the church."

By creating standards that seem extreme to the outsider, Pentecostals create boundaries between themselves and others. They recognize that in so doing they often create negative images that are difficult to combat. The balance between "different" and "freakish" is not an easy one to maintain. Yet, when others find them weird and extreme, that serves to draw attention to the group as well. In fact, by creating a group image that is so clearly the antithesis of modern America, they are also establishing a mechanism for the defense of the group.

Dress is only one aspect of the Pentecostal comment on and public rejection of the evils of the world. The rejection by Pentecostals of such all-American activities as movies, ball games, card-playing, liquor drinking, dancing, swearing, and television viewing can cause a good deal of resentment on the part of those who swear, go to movies, and love ball games, cards, drinking, and dancing. It is an open attack on American life and a Pentecostal comment on what they see as the debauchery and squalor in most Americans' lives. As with their dress, Pentecostals use their own rejection of the ways of the world as a comment on the sad lives of the people "in the world" and as a means of enhancing their own sense of group identity at the same time. Outsiders are often intimidated by the exclusive nature of the Pentecostal community, its devotion to the church, rejection of worldly matters, and the incredible sense of family and mutual support it conveys. Historically, asceticism on any level has been met by nonascetics with admiration for the diligent self-sacrificer as well as with enmity, stemming from jealousy and feelings of inadequacy.

Pentecostals do not participate in the world because they believe they have been given the special status of knowing the truth and having the promise of salvation. One young Pentecostal articulates how believers manipulate stereotypes: "Everyone looked at Pentecost as an uneducated, misinformed people, underprivileged. That was what Pentecost was represented as. They were people who had nothing else to go to except this weird religion. . . . But God had to find a people that wanted him above anything else. . . . And he got that people and he grew them into a beautiful family that would turn around and tell the world what we've got is the message for the end time."

Because Pentecostals have been given an order by God to witness to non-believers and try to convert them before "the end time," dress and deportment take on special significance within the Pentecostal community. The life of a "Saint" (a Pentecostal believer) is a model and a witness to all who might observe that life. Saints have a duty to act like saints at all times. They must be prepared to go out into the world, but they must never join the world or participate in it under penalty of hell and rejection by Jesus. Being a model begins very early for the Pentecostal believer. The following story illustrates how Pentecostal mothers convey to their children the seriousness of their actions. "And my first son, probably one of his biggest disappointments was he came in and said, 'Well, next week is the prom and I'm going.' And I said, 'All right, you can. Fine, it's all right. You go to the prom, Tony,' and I said, 'but I want to talk to you about it a little bit.' And I go upstairs and said, 'You know you can't go to the prom and play your trumpet in church. Now, you're welcome to go to the prom, but you cannot grace the front of the church, anymore, if you go.' And he said, 'All right.' And he didn't go, and I was real proud of him." Of course, the boy is not actually "welcome" to go to the dance. He fully understands the implications of what his mother says to him. If he goes, he is not a good model to others and it would be wrong, therefore, for him to "grace the front of the church" and play his trumpet in some sort of pretense that he is a model Pentecostal.

Pentecostals are acutely aware that many people think of Pentecostalism as a "cult," and in recent years believers have had to fight what they view as an unpleasant stereotype. The belief that Pentecostals are dangerous is reinforced by the evangelistic nature of their faith. For many non-Pentecostals, the constant, public proselytizing of Pentecostals is an affront. Pentecostals are often perceived as pushy, brash, and intolerant of other viewpoints. For the Pentecostal, however, evangelizing is a duty. Theirs is not a religion to keep under lock and key; it is not possible to sit back and rest serene in the knowledge of sure salvation. Pentecostals believe they are under direct orders from God to save as many souls as they can. They take this commission very seriously, fully aware of the animosity that arises from their persistence. But, again, this only serves to further unite them in their evangelistic mission. "Did you get rejected today by the man at work? Do you tire of the ridicule you receive as you try to spread God's word?" questions a Pentecostal preacher as he reassures his flock that "God knows how hard we're trying. Bug that guy until you break him down. He'll thank you in the end." Perseverance in the face of distrust, dislike, and ridicule brings Pentecostals closer together as a group.

Pentecostal dress, rejection of the world and persistent proselytizing all contribute to a "holier than thou" attitude that is difficult for outsiders to accept, but is generally cultivated with pride within the ranks of Pentecostals. It is, in fact, one of the most effective means of creating importance for a group. Sacrifice, martyrdom, self-denial and abnegation are easy routes to self-aggrandizement and shared conceptions of worth. Discourse to this effect pervades Pentecostal church services and must be recognized as a primary benefit for persons seeking feelings of self-worth, as well as for the part it plays in establishing group identity. Even so, Pentecostals are not unaware of the negative effect this attitude can have on others, including potential converts, and may try to offset it. "For a long time people looked at Pentecost and they thought, 'Oh, you're too holy to touch,' but that's not the truth, that's not the way it is."

Even more than nonconformist dress, rejection of the world, and persistent evangelizing, Pentecostal religious behavior has drawn the animosity of outsiders. Pentecostal church services are characterized as wild, frenetic, crazy, unbelievable, immoral, unseemly, vulgar, emotional, uncontrollable, and dangerous, especially when attendance reaches into the hundreds. Ecstatic religious behavior is all the more difficult to comprehend when placed in juxtaposition with the holy asceticism Pentecostals embrace. While their dress and rejection of the world may have earned for them the "holier-than-thou" accusation, their charismatic religious behavior has earned them the epithet "Holy Rollers." Although Pentecostals are aware of the widespread use of the term, it is not a term they have adopted for themselves, even though they openly condone and strive for the expressive, uninhibited behaviors exhibited in their services. "People call the Pentecostals 'Holy Rollers.' It came from when people would get converted, you know, some of them, not all of them, rolled on the floor, and they called everybody then 'Holy Rollers.' I definitely resented that. I didn't like that. I didn't think that maybe everybody don't receive their baptism the same."

This same woman, in describing the conversion of her husband, related: "And they said, 'Oh, your husband's getting the Holy Ghost, come down here.' And when I walked in the room it was just full of light, a radiant light in that room and some of the brothers was praying with my husband and when I opened the door, I guess God planned this for me to see, but my husband was just knocked backwards just like somebody knocked him down because the power of God was so strong in that room."

Suggestions of mass hysteria, possession behaviors, and trance-like states of tongue-speakers may be associated in many people's minds with primitive religious behaviors and feared and rejected for that reason. On the other hand, the New Testament basis for tongue-speaking as evidence of possession by the Holy Ghost makes a lot of Christians nervous: what if the Pentecostals are right? This may, in part, account for the current interest in the seeking of "tongues" by many charismatic groups in mainline denomination churches. These groups are often not openly condoned by the hierarchy of the churches, but many non-Pentecostal Christians and pastors are convinced of the reality of the tongue-speaking experience. This should not, however, suggest an improvement of the non-Pentecostal public opinion of Pentecostal behavior. On the con-

trary, very clear distinctions are made between modern charismatics (pentecostal with a lowercase "p") and Pentecostalism. Charismatics generally emphasize the quiet, intellectual nature of their evening meetings, held perforce in homes rather than in the church proper. The Holy Spirit is gently wooed through quiet individual prayer and testimony; connotations of "Pentecostalism" or loud, raucous meetings are vociferously denied and discouraged.

Pentecostals, of course, view recent trends toward charismatic experience as supportive of their own beliefs. Yet, they are critical of the reserved nature of the denominational charismatics and look with disdain upon what they see as elite reluctance to admit emotionalism and "irrationality," both of which they feel are necessary components of true religious experience. One Pentecostal woman put it this way: "I think shouting is great and people on the outside don't understand that because they haven't already received the real joy, and they don't have their eyes set on the eternity that we have a hope for. When you think about it, and you think about what we are going to escape and what we're going to receive, it is a joy and it is something to shout about. People don't think a thing about going to a ball game and screaming and yelling and getting down on their hands and beating the ground and beating the floor. They think that's all right."

Her point is well taken. Americans have decided that quiet decorum is appropriate for church services and that sports arenas are proper places for exuberant, loud, uninhibited behavior. It is not, therefore, Pentecostal behavior so much that dismays outsiders as the association of that behavior with religious ecstasy and religious emotionalism. For believers, however, Pentecostal religious frenzy, established and maintained as a mechanism for group identity and boundary maintenance, might be explained to outsiders this way: "What I am trying to say is for so long we walked around with it, 'Hey, we've got it. We've got the answer for the world.' And we've become an unreal people. And it is time for them to see that we have got joy. That we are real people. We act crazy. . . . We're nuts for Jesus and we are happy about it."

The non-Pentecostal response to Pentecostals has been unflattering. When fear, intimidation, awe, and awkwardness come together in one group's notions about another group, the likely outcome will be ridicule and persecution. Although Pentecostals feel the same fear, intimidation, awe, and awkwardness about the non-Pentecostal world, their status is the slighter because they are the minority group. Ever since the advent of emotional revivals and camp meetings, Pentecostals have suffered at the hands of outsiders. Persecution and ostracism are bitter realities for most Pentecostals, and the stories they tell often include incidents in which they were made to feel ridiculous, embarrassed, and defensive about their religion. But persecution is also a powerful force for uniting people and facilitating cohesion. Pentecostals decry their persecution and vow their perseverance. Church services resound with the testimonies of believers who have been belittled, and the congregation rallies to their support. The overwhelming response to Sister Connie's testimony was a testament to the deeply felt cohesion of the group:

> *You know when I sing*
> *And when I testify*
> *Everybody looks at me*
> *And they think I'm kind of* peculiar.
> *But you know tonight*
> *We* are peculiar people!
> *But you know something?*
> *I'm not ashamed of Jesus,*
> *Because this is the Lord,*
> *That I sing*

That I testify for
That I stomp my feet for
That I clap my hands for
It's Jesus Christ.

When the congregation responds with "Amen, yes, Sister," they are in one accord. They, as a group, have been misunderstood and mistreated, but it is exactly that identification as a group which helps to bind them together. They are proud that they are peculiar, for that means they have established a distinct identity.

Although Pentecostals are not comfortable with being called "Holy Rollers," they are inadvertently effective in perpetuating the popular beliefs about their religion that are reflected in the name. Their own stories about Pentecostal behavior are not told as sensationalized accounts of bizarre behavior, but rather are carefully constructed, nearly formulaic personal experience stories reiterated to contrast an outsider's view with an insider's view. The telling of conversion stories, especially, serves to define boundaries from an inside point of view and interpret behavior within the context in which it occurs. The effect, then, is to solidify the stereotype as an esoteric conviction. The stories begin on a definite outsider note.

This typical story, describing how one couple felt about Pentecostals before their own conversion, was told to non-Pentecostals: "He, my husband, would come in and say, 'Well, where do you want to go, let's go to church.' And I would say, 'Well, where do you want to go?' . . . And he said to me, 'I tell you, I'll go anywhere you want to go but don't expect me to go up on that hill. . . . Don't expect me to go up there. Those people are crazy and you do not have to live like that to be a Christian.' " At the insistence of the woman's sister and her husband, this couple did go to the Pentecostal church and joined the church within a few nights. Then, the woman defended Pentecostals; the outsider stance had changed to an insider's—"People think we are freaks, but really we're not." The "they" has become "we."

Their daughter-in-law describes her first encounter with Pentecostals; this account also is typical: "My girlfriend and I when we first entered into this Pentecostal church, this is kinda going back, I remember seeing the people raising their hands and speaking in tongues and one little lady shouting and we sat back there and I would just laugh, because I thought this was really unreal. . . . And when I seen these people clapping their hands and raising their hands to worship the Lord, I thought this is, you know, this is really out of place for them to do this in church. Church is to come and sit still."

Although these descriptions of uncomfortable first encounters with Pentecostals are quickly followed by comments about the converts' changing attitudes toward what was first perceived, the account of the first encounter serves a critical function. This part of the conversion narration is easily empathized with by all the outsiders listening—it describes exactly how they are feeling as newcomers, observers, and outsiders. In essence, the believer is announcing, "I know how you feel at this moment and yours is a legitimate feeling; I felt the same way." The recounting of the conversion then leads the outsider toward an understanding of what he or she should expect to happen next. Skepticism will recede as God reveals to each individual the reality of what is occurring in the service. Signs will be sought to prove the legitimacy of the experience. The outsider comes to see that the people are not freakish at all, but rather have found "the Truth."

> The second night after that I came back because I thought I would laugh again . . . and I realized it was more than just watching people, that they really did have something that they were expressing and that it was real. . . . I knew there

> was something there and I knew it was right. How I could reach out and get it, I did not know. So I watched these people and after a while I started crying . . . and then I received the Holy Ghost and I forgot all about my make-up and forgot all about my pride . . . and then I just started praising the Lord.

Once nonbelievers go through the experience of "receiving the Holy Ghost" and speak in tongues, they become group members and the benefits are multifold. It is the public display of tongue-speaking that entitles a person to membership in the Pentecostal Family: "It's a family, it is just like a family. It really is. And you are concerned for your brother and sisters. . . . You have a desire to help your brothers and sisters, and it is a definite family thing. Really, I think in some of the 'denominational' churches, they don't have that closeness and it is the Holy Ghost, the difference is the Holy Ghost that covers that, I think." There is no tie stronger, more resistant to breakage, more filled with a sense of devotion and loyalty against all odds than the tie of blood-related people. Pentecostals believe they are blood-related to each other, through the blood of Jesus Christ. They are brothers and sisters; they belong to a family. They understand what they do and why they do it, and they stand as a group against a world that does not understand, taking the outsider's stereotypes about them to mold an image that is stronger against opposition.

Finally, much of the Pentecostal belief system, as well as their own perceptions of themselves as a group, are firmly embodied in a specialized language they have developed. Generally, the use of this specialized language by Pentecostals does not create contention or distrust on the part of nonbelievers, because its use is largely confined to the religious church service and the Pentecostal community. But within the group, the special language functions in a significant manner to establish a group sense of cohesion and special identity and should be examined in any discussion of Pentecostals as a folk group. Words and phrases that have developed naturally within the Pentecostal community are fraught with meaning and carry significance not available to the nonmember.

Folk groups and subcultures often develop a specialized language understood only by the members of the group, a language that must be learned as a new member becomes assimilated into the group and that, when artfully and correctly employed, will signify membership to others in the group. Specialized language serves further to mark the group to outsiders, to delineate boundaries that keep groups distinct, and to intensify group cohesion and solidarity. A special language must be close enough to the mother language to make sense to the members of the group and simple enough for the novice to pick up fairly quickly. No time is set aside for the teaching of this specialized language, but its constant and repetitive use in the verbal messages of the group members serves to teach the newcomer what the words mean and where and how it is appropriate to employ them. Converts to Pentecostalism are expected to participate fully in church services immediately upon their conversion and tongue-speaking experience; hence, acquisition of the language quickly follows initiation.

Pentecostal converts generally come from the community in which the Pentecostal church has established itself, and are brought in by "fervent and convincing recruitment along pre-existing lines of significant social relationships."[5] The conversion of neighbors will stabilize the church community and help it to grow; conversion of loners and drifters will not really benefit the group. In southern Indiana, relatives, close friends and neighbors of Pentecostal believers acquire familiarity with the Pentecostal language long before they join the group themselves. Pentecostal believers tell many stories that artfully employ the language they have acquired within the religion. Much of the language and its proper use is learned in the context of the church service, but the employment of the specialized language and the accompanying stories go beyond the church into the homes, the stores, the schools, in fact, into the entire community. Therefore, when a community member becomes a convert, the assimilation process is abbreviated because of his or her consistent exposure to the world of Pentecostals outside the context of the church.

No manual of Pentecostal words and their meanings exists. Many of the words or phrases common to Pentecostals have originated in the Bible but have come to carry specialized meanings for the people who employ them. Some of the terms are esoteric enough that outsiders are not likely to know what they mean—for example, when Pentecostals speculate about the impending *rapture* (when Jesus will return to gather up believers). Other terms serve also to articulate the difference between Pentecostals and outsiders—for example, the Pentecostal use of the terms *saint* and *sinner*. Interestingly, when Pentecostals talk with non-Pentecostals they assume a common knowledge of their specialized language, or at least they employ it with no pause for explanation. It is such an integral part of their own vocabulary that I am quite certain they are not aware that some of their language might give an outsider difficulties. The Pentecostal terms that follow have definitions that have developed within the group—in some cases, unique definitions applicable only in the Pentecostal context. Some of the terms are also used in other Christian groups, but in this examination of specialized religious language I shall try to illustrate the nuance of meaning that comes from the use of the term within the Pentecostal setting.

Pentecostals, like some other Christians, call each other *Brother* and *Sister*, but for Pentecostals this tradition has special meaning. Because they do feel they are literally a family, these terms are not mere titles but are imbued with a greater intensity of meaning: "The Pentecostal church as a whole is a very, is kind of a familial feel. We call each other brothers and sisters and we are brothers and sisters. . . . There is definitely a feeling of kinship among each other."

The most significant esoteric differentiation between Pentecostal group members and nonmembers is the in-group use of the terms *saint* and *sinner*. Sinners are people who are *out in the world*, a phrase that is used to describe the world of sin in which Pentecostals do not participate but the rest of the world does. Sinners commit sins; they do things that are worldly: these include going to movies, dances, any kind of commercial amusement activities, paid sports events, bars, in fact any place, including other homes, where the influence of the world might be evident—this includes television. Pentecostals call themselves, on the other hand, saints. They have been saved; that is, through their conversion they will be saved from an eternity in hell. The Pentecostal church is made up of saints; often the congregation is addressed as "Dear Saints." Sinners seeking to change their status from sinner to saint and gain membership in the group must do so by first professing their sins in the public context of the church and *tarrying* at the altar, that is, waiting at the altar (on bended knee) for the possession of the Holy Ghost. The kinesic language that accompanies tarrying includes raised arms, waving hands, closed eyes, tears, and the eventual disconnection from one's surroundings that implies a trance state. Possession by the Holy Ghost will be manifested by *speaking in tongues*, a linguistic phenomenon that Pentecostals believe is often an example of a true language, understandable to people familiar with it. The tarrying may take minutes or hours, or the potential convert may have to return night after night trying to *pray through*—that is, to reach God. This process can be completed on the first night or may take years. *Seekers*, the ones who tarry, are encouraged by saint helpers to *let go* and *go all the way with Jesus*—to get rid of all their inhibitions. Members generally attribute the inattention of the Holy Ghost to some lack of faith or indecision on the part of the seeker.

In order to become a saint, a sinner must be baptized twice—once by immersion in water, and again *in the spirit*, which means she or he receives the Holy Ghost and speaks in tongues. Once a sinner has confessed her or his sins and requested baptism, the pastor of the church will baptize this person in water. Pentecostal baptism is accompanied by a standardized prayer, the quoting of a Bible verse, and often tongue-speaking by the pastor or another church member. Oneness Pentecostals water baptize with the following formula: "I now baptize you in the name of Jesus." They have rejected the long-standing Christian formula for baptism—"I now baptize thee in the name of the Father, the Son, and the Holy Ghost"—preferring instead to recognize only Jesus as the Godhead incarnate. To other Christians, including other Pentecostals, this seems inaccurate and ineffective. Membership in this group, based on both baptisms (water and spirit), assures salvation and safety in heaven when the *rapture* comes. The rapture will be when Jesus returns to the earth to claim his saints and all persons will be held accountable for their lives and deeds. Pentecostals believe the rapture is imminent; the impending doom will be, of course, followed by the millennium. Their enforced rejection of the world makes their anticipation of the better life after the rapture all important: "We have so many things to do, realizing that the place that we are at, in these times, coming down to the end, when I really feel the rapture of the church is ready to take place. I expect it tonight, if it doesn't take place tonight, I expect it tomorrow. And there's such a short time that we have to witness to other people to let them know what they can receive and the change that can take place in their lives."

Spontaneous tongue-speaking, at events such as baptisms, is distinct in the Pentecostal mind from that which occurs in a conversion experience. Being able to speak in tongues, following the initial tongue-speaking experience, is a *gift* and is generally recognized by believers as a message from God. Saints may possess special spiritual gifts from God. According to 1 Corinthians 12, the nine spiritual gifts include wisdom, knowledge, faith, healing, working of miracles, prophecy, discerning of spirits, speaking in divers tongues, and the interpretation of tongues. Pentecostals interpret these verses to indicate that God decides which (if any) of these gifts will be given to whom. Speaking in divers tongues refers to speaking in tongues under inspiration in various appropriate situations; this ability is seen as a gift and is recognized as different from the spontaneous, but involuntary, tongue-speaking that accompanies a conversion experience, which is believed to be available to everyone and is a prerequisite to membership in the group: "I think, as far as the gifts, receiving the Holy Ghost and speaking in tongues, and then I think there is a gift of tongues which are two separate things altogether. Some people have the gift of tongues and some don't. I feel that probably my husband has a gift of tongues. He has prayed in many other languages that were went from one just into another and I don't feel that everybody has that gift." The *interpretation* of what someone "says" in tongues is thought to be the highest gift of all but is rarely practiced, for it is agreed that interpreting is subject to the greatest risk; the burden of a mistaken interpretation lies with the interpreter, whereas the tongue-speaker is possessed and is not responsible for what is spoken.

In a typical Pentecostal church service several activities are common, all of which are geared toward helping the group members *get happy* or *get a blessing*, which refers to states where uninhibited behaviors such as crying, *dancing in the spirit* (in possession), jerks, tongue-speaking, and shouting can be exhibited. *Shouting* can take various forms, from shrieking to crying to speaking in tongues. It is viewed as a supranormal utterance, and, like spirit dancing, cannot be controlled by the individual. This marks the distinction between such behaviors as secular activities and as sacred activities performed in the context of the church service. Under the power of the spirit of God, the saints are not responsible for their acts; performed by choice in the context of the "world," the same acts become desecrated. Participation in congregational singing, dancing, shouting, praying, and tongue-speaking is strongly encouraged; saints long to see *the house on fire* for God, that is, all members actively involved in exalting God and invoking the spirit to move among the members.

Testifying is one verbal activity that all members are expected to perform within any given church service; a member is expected rise at the pew and give an extemporaneous testimony of faith in God or God's particular goodness to him or her. Testifying is part of the duty of a good saint. Personal experience stories serve to witness for the Lord; the act of testifying itself is a witness of the saint's effort to be a good model for others.

Knowledge of the specialized language of Pentecostals is attained in a traditional manner, passed from group member to group member, both in the church and in the community. Many Pentecostals relate stories about growing up in Pentecostal homes and playing church. "Most of my friends were people that was in the church. When I was little my parents would go to visit every Saturday night. They would go places or would have people to their homes and we played church. . . . That was part of the games we played. And one little guy he always did the preaching and he always tried to get me to get the Holy Ghost." Stories such as this reveal the pervading influence of the Pentecostal religion on the lives of its adherents. Most of their friends were Pentecostal; friends visited each other's homes in the evenings, the same friends they saw at church on other evenings; children "played church." The language used in these stories suggests that the children, even at a very early age, were cognizant of and competent with Pentecostal terminology and behavior.

In a given community, Pentecostals do constitute a folk group. Their sense of identity as a group is a complex of sociocultural configurations that have developed naturally, yet are unconsciously manipulated by the members to solidify group cohesion and maintain distinctions between them and everybody else. Pentecostals have set themselves up as being different from the rest of the world; they have established dress codes and a specialized language to mark that distinction. In their efforts to be recognized as different, they have suffered the consequences of ridicule, misunderstanding, and persecution. Their differentness is most often perceived by outsiders as freakish, bizarre, and even dangerous. Yet, most of the stereotypes about Pentecostals create little apprehension for the adherents of the faith, for they have learned to turn a negative stereotype into a positive attribute, a fearful connotation into an exaltation of their God. Unlike the Amish or other isolated religious communities within the modern American milieu, Pentecostals mingle daily with other groups in their world. Yet, close observation and examination of the attitudes and behaviors of Pentecostals reveals that, in many ways, Pentecostals have created similar marks of distinction and have established and continue to maintain sociocultural boundaries important to their distinctiveness as a group. Like ethnic groups, they have a membership that identifies itself, is identifiable by others, and has a cultural focus of one or more symbolic elements defined as the epitome of their religious peoplehood.

CHAPTER THREE

Discourse Rules

Oh, I can remember when we'd go to church and get home about one or two in the morning. I just don't think they paid as much attention to the time really. And I can remember when we used to have prayer meetings, well, maybe we'd have altar call for an hour or two. Folks would pray that hard and long.

HIGHWAY 341, a "B" paved road, traverses Indiana from north to south, winding its way down to Bedford, the "Limestone Capital of the World." On a long stretch, where houses appear infrequently and state forests brood on both sides of the hilly, curving road, a tiny handmade sign on the left, easy to miss, points down a dirt road—"Johnson's Creek Church." The road immediately dips low, then curves sharply away from the highway and crawls through private fields, passing rambling farm houses, now in poor repair, with kids and dogs running down the hill precariously close to the road.

Even when you have found this church numerous times before, it always feels as though those three slow miles are wrong and you've passed it already or someone stole the church in the middle of the night. Then, standing stark, flanked by tiny wooden outhouses to each side, a small, plain white church comes into view. The fallow fields, still scarred by last year's planting furrows, stretch in all directions away from the bare hard-packed dirt space reserved for cars and pickups. Trucks pull up with their bumpers touching the rails of the wooden front steps and teen-agers sit on the hood, laughing, waiting for church to begin, or dragging guitars and amplifiers from the truck beds, electric cords trailing behind. An old Chevy pulls up at right angles to the church and parks in front of the steps; thirty-seven people young and old seem to tumble out of its doors, sending greetings to those who hold open the door and bring in the instruments.

The people arriving at this church could be folks from nearby Heltonville or Stinesville, even from Bedford, though most live not far down the dirt road. Most are women, driving cars, bringing their mothers and their grandmothers, their sisters and their sisters' kids. These are plain women with long, braided hair and longer dresses, freely giving hugs all around, murmuring "Praise the Lord" and "God Bless You" to each in turn. Sometimes the hugs are long ones and the women touch each other's hair, their faces, to wipe away the tears: the worry of a sick child, an aging parent, or a jobless husband. Few words are necessary, for each woman knows the story of each of the other women. I can only guess what they know about each other.

Johnson's Creek Church is a typical rural Pentecostal church—a white wooden structure, with three wooden steps leading up to a single metal storm door that opens the wrong way and tries to knock you off the precarious steps. Inside is a single large room, simple in design. No double doors or vestibule greet the newcomer; the door opens abruptly into the sanctuary. Here, we find bare wooden floors and no more than fifteen or twenty hard wooden pews, without benefit of pads or upholstery. The windows, four on each side, are adorned only with plain white window shades and are wide open to the night air. An enormous oscillating fan sits in the back corner and hums noisily, forcing hot air onto the backs of the congregation. Evidence of an old chimney can still be seen on one wall, its stovepipe hole covered with a tin of Jesus Blessing the Little Children. A depiction of the Last Supper, on black velvet, reigns from the front of the room, directly behind the pulpit; another portrait of a gentle, long-haired Jesus with lambs hangs to the left of the pulpit. In the corners stand a Christian flag and an American flag. The pulpit stands on a bare wooden platform elevated about four inches off the floor. There is no altar, no prayer or communion bench. The plain wooden pulpit is flanked by a small piano to the congregation's right and several haphazardly placed chairs to their left. A wooden "Church Register" announces 140 members, 42 in attendance last Sunday, 56 last week, and an offering of $32.16. There is no baptistry, no choir loft, no organ, no microphone.

As the group gathers outside the doors of the church, young musicians begin to choose their places in the folding chairs to the left of the pulpit. Anyone who plays an instrument can join this band, although many more males play than do women. Rhythm instruments are the most popular, but different nights will see different instruments. Usually there are several guitars, both electric and acoustic, a banjo, sometimes a drum set, perhaps an accordion; tambourines lie about on the pews for anyone to play. Some of the older men who play the harmonica may prefer to sit in their pews and play from there. All of these musicians are congregation members; most of them cannot read any music at all. They only play in the church service because they enjoy it. The pastor may, on occasion, ask one of them to play and sing a "special," but such a request is usually spontaneous and unrehearsed.

It is still light outside as sounds of the tuning instruments reach our ears and float out across the now greying fields. Then, the music is loud, pulsating, calling us in for service. Apparently without being asked, but perhaps subtly prodded, a woman climbs onto the platform and stands behind the pulpit, exclaiming how glad she is to be in the house of God again tonight, and begins the service with a bouncy chorus or a hymn from the book, as the musicians and congregation stumble, trying to catch and follow her song. For several hours, then, men and women perform an entire service that is rich in oral tradition: the singing, the praying, the testifying, the preaching, the healing, the speaking in tongues are all enacted according to the prevailing rules of this congregation and delivered before the congregation for critique and appreciation.[1]

The Pentecostal religious service is a stage for several different levels of performed verbal art. Although the services appear to the uninitiated to be disjointed and not obedient to any organizational rules, they are, in fact, quite controlled and do follow internal rules of appropriateness for performed acts, actors, and evaluation—rules that have been established and are maintained along informal, traditional lines through several generations of believers. Who can perform which acts, when, and from what positions within the context of the service are rules established within the sociocultural matrix of this religious community. Before it is possible to discern what those rules are, it is first necessary to analyze a typical religious service.

The analysis I shall present is based on over a hundred hours of recorded services at Johnson's Creek Church. I have recorded many hours of services from numerous other Pentecostal churches in the same area and have concluded that each church community establishes an order for its services and appropriate rules for verbal discourse within that order. The order and rules are different and specific for each church community, reflecting the makeup of that particular congregation, its needs, and the traditions it has created and fostered. It is a critical error to lump white or black Protestants together or to describe "Pentecostal sects," "fundamentalists," or an idealized "folk church" in general. Each church will exhibit some of the traditional forms that characterize a folk church, but these forms will be manifested in particular ways that have developed within the context of that specific church group; unique patterns of discourse will also reflect the concerns of subtly different theological stances and beliefs about encounters with the supernatural. What can be said, how, when, by whom, and in what manner are established and maintained by the group. Yet, even within traditional, formulaic constructs, individual creativity is possible and allowed as long as it appears in sanctioned positions within the event and as long as the goals and ends are along group lines.

Recent trends in folkloristics have led us to acknowledge both contextual relevance and performance rules in addition to actual verbatim text when examining instances of verbal art. Performance-centered folkloristics examines the "interactional setting of display behavior" as well as "the situated meaning of performance forms."[2] Attention to and respect for the ethnography of communication have raised awareness of the need to look to the concerns of the community in which the performances occur for clues to their meaning. Firmly implanting performances in the context in which they naturally occur and charting the codes used and manipulated by performers and judged by audiences in specific examples of "display behavior" will reveal the concerns of the speakers, the breadth of shared experience of the group, and the sociocultural matrix of the verbal, proxemic, kinesic, and semiotic behaviors.

Pentecostals assert that "anything" can happen at any time in a church service; they eschew the notion of a church bulletin that outlines the order of a service because this does not allow the spirit of God full rein in the service. It is just such audacity on the part of other Christians, they feel, that has prevented their services from being spirit-filled. *He* must be in control at all times, they say, not humans. There is often mention in the service of the importance of a flexibility of order, the implication that the service might go on all night if the Lord "takes over." Nonetheless, there is discernible order to the events that occur in any given service. Even though there is a strong stated belief that the spirit can affect a person at any time, close attention to the actual events and how the components within the events are manipulated supports the reality that, in fact, behaviors have been carefully relegated to appropriate positions within the event—the spirit is consciously wooed only at certain points and in particular ways.

In the analysis that follows I shall refer to a single service as *the speech situation,* the frames for differential speech within that situation as *speech events,* and the components of the events as *speech acts.*[3] I shall be concerned with delineating the frames in which these acts are likely to be found to discern how frames overlap, and to determine the co-occurrence rules for speech acts from frame to frame.[4]

In order to ascertain that there is order to these services it has been important to separate the segments of the service and compartmentalize verbal genres within those segments. The tables included in this chapter attempt to graphically illustrate the many components of a complex religious event. Table 1 is the most complex of the tables in its delineation of all the verbal constituents in the speech situation: the likely participants, the message (its form, goals, and outcomes), and the various interactional rules of discourse and performance.[5] A typical religious service will first be described in a general manner; the reader is invited to relate each segment of the described service to the corresponding line in table 1. A discussion of the native or emic, that is, Pentecostal, verbal genres of Pentecostals as well as further necessary explication of table 1 will follow the general description.[6] Tables 2, 3, and 4 provide examination of certain aspects of verbal performances within the structure of the religious service.

Each service at Johnson's Creek is preceded by a greeting ceremony (a speech event), which consists of all participants shaking hands with strangers and "saints," and always offering the greetings "Praise the Lord" and "God Bless You." This greeting ceremony concludes when someone goes to the front, stands behind the pulpit, and begins a chorus or asks the group to turn to a particular page in the hymnal.

As the musicians find their places and tune their instruments, congregation members begin to move slowly toward the church building. One musician may simply begin a bouncy religious tune and the others will pick it up, or someone will yell out a suggested song for them all to begin playing. When they do, it serves to announce to those both inside and out that the service is about to begin. Folks inside, already in their pews, may begin clapping to the loud music; some may even dance in the area between the first pew and the band. Most of the favorite songs of Johnson's Creek are not songs found in their hymnals but choruses they have learned orally in the religious context over the years. Many of these songs are traditional and recognizable in many different versions. They are fast, vibrant, catchy, short songs that are easy to learn, easy to clap to, dance to, and add to:

> I'm going over Jordan to see my mother
> I'm going over Jordan to see my mother
> I'm going over Jordan to see my mother
> Glorious day, oh, glorious day.

Other verses include "going over Jordan to see my father," to "see my brother," to "see my sister." This chorus lends itself easily, too, to personal additions. Thus, one could "line out" for the congregation "I'm going over Jordan to see my daughter," and the group would comply with the rest of the verse. Favored songs are those with a good beat and the flexibility for repeated verses. Some favorite choruses might be sung as many as twenty or thirty times without variation as well. The key is to keep the level of intensity as high as possible; loud, continuous, rhythmic music will serve this purpose. This portion of the song service may

Table 1
SCHEMA OF COMPONENTS OF SPEECH ACTS

ACT SITUATION		*ACT SEQUENCE*		*PARTICIPANTS*			*ENDS*
SCENE	SETTING	MESSAGE FORM	MESSAGE CONTENT	SENDER	RECEIVER	AUDIENCE	GOALS
(FRAME) Greeting Time	Outside church; church entrance; inside church before service begins	Formulaic Greeting	"Praise the Lord"	Group Member	Other group members; non-members	Receiver of Greeting	Make arrivals feel welcome; human contact
Singing	Inside church; begins service; singers in pews	Songs from hymnals	Heaven will be better; we are heaven bound; Jesus is your friend; the joy of being "saved;" abolishment of loneliness; power of prayer	All attenders in unison	All present	Song leader; pastor	Begin service; create "spirited" mood
Praying	Inside church	Petitions to God	Prayer for "lost" souls, sick or backsliden members; for daily support of Jesus in dealing with life and lures of "the world;" for God to enter service	All members in unison	God		To make life easier by placing responsibility in God's hands
"Specials" (singing)	Inside church	Personal favorite gospel songs; country-western tunes with words written by group members	Heavenbound and heaven is a better place; life will be better later; keep the faith; Jesus is your friend	Group members	Congregation; preachers	Entire congregation	To entertain
Testifying	Inside church;	Short to medium length "speech"	(Meta) prayer for privilege of being in church (I want to thank God for...); persuasive rhetoric designed to convince others to join group (witnessing); formal testament to God's influence on life; request for prayer by other members for own proper behavior	One member at a time; usually	Other members; non-members	Other members; testimony leader; pastor	Have personal statements serve as models for proper behavior; admonish; teach; relate life to religion
Preaching	Inside church; final segment of "formal" service design	Long "speech"	Live for God; reward is heaven—punishment is hell; heaven will be better; don't sin, be good Pentecostals; stick together; witness for Jesus; be a model for others	Usually one man	Members Non-members, usually women	Members, usually women	Direct members; recruit new members; perpetuate faith; encourage enthusiasm and participation
Altar Call	Begins inside church but may end with people drifting out—no set closing	Admonitions from Pastor to surrender to God and seek Holy Ghost in order to be saved from eternity in hell	Heaven is only for those who speak in tongues; Members are told to seek a blessing (speak in tongues); Uninhibited behavior urged with "Let go", "Give in", "Submit yourself"	Pastor, male	Members, Non-members, usually female	All present; members, usually female	Get members and nonmembers to participate in uninhibited behaviors

ENDS		*INSTRUMENTALITIES*		*NORMS*		
OUTCOMES	KEY	CHANNELS	FORMS OF SPEECH	OF INTERACTION	OF INTERPRETATION	GENRES
Newcomers relax; Members feel part of the group	Friendly; sincere and soft-spoken	Normal speaking voice	Formula	Smiles; handshakes; hugs; kisses; pats on body—all reciprocated among members; generally accepted shyly by non-members	Brotherhood-Sisterhood expressed and desired; group believed to be "family of God"	Ritual Greeting
Group participation; service begins to "liven up"	Joyful; loud; intense; sincere; happy	Sung (accompanied by electric instruments, drums, tamborines); chanted; shouted	Rhymed lines/ formulas from hymnals	Members stand or sit facing front of church; song leader faces congregation from podium; all may clap; raise hands; dance; march	Loud singing honors God; dancing in spirit, marching, shouting all signs of God's presence in church	Song
Sense of security; peace of mind; relinquished responsibility for what will or may happen	Intense; sincere; low-key or may be loud; penitent	Spoken in normal voice; chanted; moaned	Formulas; exhortations; extemporaneous discourse; unintelligible sounds; shouts	Members kneel at pews or at altar with heads down and usually eyes closed; or head in hands; pastor kneels behind podium, usually with head in one hand	Time of direct address to God; sincerity and faith believed to get results	Prayer
Congregation is pleased; others volunteer to sing	Friendly; dutiful and cooperative; sincere	Sung (accompanied by piano and/or guitar	Rhymed line formulas put to music	Singers gather around piano and sing for seated congregation; are applauded at finish	Singing honors God; members are duty-bound to sing; treated by group as entertainment segment of service	Song
Stage is set for responses and other testimonies; emotional mood set; people do speak in tongues and dance in the spirit	Sincere; intense; low-key to very loud; pleading; emotional	Normal speaking voice; or fast, clipped; chanted; sung; shouted	Formulas; exhortations; extemporaneous discourse; recitation of Bible verses; recitation of song verses; (meta) prayers; tag questions; exempla; personal experience stories	Speaker stands alone at pew, facing only testimony leader and pastor; speaker may end by shouting and dancing—or may invoke others to do so; reaction to one testimony must reside before another begins	Expression of faith; dutiful participation in service; proof of submission to spirit of God	Testimony
Educates; explicates; inculcates norms; excites; chastizes	Sincere; intense; loud; cajoling; pleading	Normal speaking voice; chanted; shouted; screamed; sung	Formulas; exhortations; extemporaneous discourse; fillers; recitation of Bible verses; rhetorical questions; shouts; exempla; personal experience stories	Preacher faces congregation from podium; he may dance, stomp, march across front platform; wave hands; point fingers	God's message in preacher's words; "excited" sermon indicates God's presence	Sermon
Members leave pews and march around church; go stand or kneel at altar; dance and jerk in the spirit; faint, fall on floor; sing; cry	Excitable and powerful; loud to soft; sincere pleading; cry	Normal speaking voice; chanted; sung; unintelligible sounds; shouted	Extemporaneous discourse; formulas; exhortations; short phrases; rhetorical questions; pleas; shouts; cries	Members and non-members kneel at altar; may hug, pat, touch each other; march around church in lines; stand in trance with hands raised; place one hand on "seeker" with other hand in air	Uninhibited behaviors sign of submission to spirit of God; God's presence indicated in bodies of those in trance-like state or speaking in tongues	-------- (part of sermon)

last from ten minutes to an hour, depending upon the needs of the people and their desire to sing.

At this point in the service, one of the pastors calls for special prayer requests and various members of the congregation mention family or community members who are sick or "lost;" the pastor then asks for a show of "silent requests" and many raise their hands for private needs. The pastor then directs the group to "go to the Lord in prayer." This is the signal for the congregation to kneel either at the front of the church or at their pews and for all to pray aloud, each person praying his or her own voluntary, spontaneous prayer. No one person leads the prayer; all are expected to participate, but when the pastor stops praying, the rest of the congregation stops praying simultaneously.

When the congregational prayer is finished, the pastor generally asks a member of the congregation to lead the testimony service. This duty also often falls to a woman. The testimony leader is expected to stand at the podium and ask for testimonies, acknowledging members as they rise to speak. It is customary for the leader to give the first testimony from the pulpit, then solicit others from the congregation. Generally, no one in the audience stands up until the leader finishes her own testimony. Courtesy rules the testimony service; no one begins speaking until the preceding person has finished. General short responses, such as "Blessed Jesus," "Thank-you, Jesus," "Thank You, Lord," or "Amen" occur throughout the testimonies. These are audience indicators of approval and often follow a member's testimony. A particularly effective testimony may elicit more dramatic participation on the part of the audience, sometimes leading to an extended period of dancing and singing in the spirit.

In most services at Johnson's Creek, ten or twelve members will testify. Testimonies may range from several seconds to half an hour. I recall the frustration of one lay preacher who recounted his unsuccessful attempt to "take on" a new church in an area close to Johnson's Creek. He lamented about a family of "loud-mouthed women" at that church who just "would not shut up"; they testified for hours, taking turns and testifying two and three times, delivering long testimonies that "dragged on and on." The church had been without a pastor for some time and the testimonies had become longer and longer. He insisted to them that the Bible directs the preacher to preach at every service, but to no avail; he could not get these women to sit down, and he finally gave up trying to be their pastor. Infrequently, testimonies will become so extended and emotional that the preacher may be unable to preach his sermon, but this occurrence is rare. Careful, subtle manipulation by the pastors generally assures that the testimony service will end when it should. Occasionally, if the testifiers are slow to speak, someone, anyone in the congregation or the testimony leader herself, may initiate a song or chorus; sometimes several choruses will be interspersed with the testimony service. Testimonies are often spurred by a song just sung and the testifier will acknowledge that the song inspired her or him to testify. The testimony service concludes when no other member stands to testify. The end is marked by the testimony leader's return to the pews and the pastor's retrieval of the pulpit.

At Johnson's Creek, the testimony service is generally followed by a series of "specials"—songs sung by small groups of the members. The pastor asks certain individuals and groups to sing, one after another. Before the evening is over, he may ask all the regular members present to sing a "special." Although admittedly one or two singers are far superior to the others, there are no established special singers; everyone is recognized as adequate to sing for the Lord. Singers usually gather around the piano and sing from private song books, not the regular hymnals. Several people in the group have their own spiral notebooks of personal favorites, which they have written out and marked for guitar or piano chords. But few, if any, can read music; the musicians play the many varied instruments entirely by ear. The special singing is brought to an end by the pastor when he determines that it has gone on long enough; the preacher for the evening's sermon is then introduced.

At Johnson's Creek Church either of the regular pastors may preach (they generally take turns service to service) or, if a preacher is visiting, she or he is generally invited to preach the sermon. This is a courtesy that is not ignored even if one of the regular pastors is fully prepared to preach. Lay preachers often travel from church to church expecting to be invited to deliver the sermon simply by virtue of their presence.

Sermons can last from twenty minutes to two hours, with the preacher often moving about in the area in front of the first pews. A good preacher who is capable of "firing up" the congregation will generally shout, cry, chant, dance, and yell at his congregation. It is expected that the audience will respond to his effective speech with exclamations such as "Amen, Brother," "Yes, Jesus," "Oh, Jesus," "Thank You, Jesus," "Thank you, Lord," and "Tell it, Brother."

Cues from the preacher to the musicians and/or to the pianist mark the end of the sermon proper and the start of the "altar call" (see table 4). The musicians begin playing soft music as the preacher winds down and begins pleading for lost souls to "come to the altar" to pray for the baptism of the Holy Ghost. Many group members may also "go to the altar" seeking a blessing—that is, hoping to go into trance and speak in tongues. The altar calls vary in their degree of success. Sometimes no one goes to the front of the church; sometimes the entire congregation finds itself there. The preacher may ask the members to join hands as they pray for the spirit to fall. If "lost" people are seeking the baptism of the spirit for the first time, members may surround them and shout encouragement, often at the same time intensifying their own excitement, which may cause them to slip into tongues and exhibit various trance-like behaviors—jerks, shouting, dancing. Generally, the music is by this time loud and pulsating, and women may be marching about the pews beating time with tambourines. This final scene may last for a few minutes or over an hour; the preacher may spend another half hour shouting and exhorting. This portion of the service cannot be segmented analytically into individual speech acts, as shouts and cries of ecstasy may come from several people simultaneously. Actions are, on the whole, uninhibited and involuntary. Members may call a halt to this phase of the service by approaching the preacher and indicating their desire to be healed. As one member receives a drop of oil from the pastor's vial upon her forehead, the other members circle her and begin to pray loudly, or shout, and some may begin to speak in tongues.

Several verbal genres appear in the Johnson's Creek Church service, and in general, these genres have more or less fixed positions within the various frames that make up the service. This church community has subdivided the larger service situation into several distinguishable smaller events: greeting time, song service, testimony service, sermon, altar call, healing service. These are the frames for the various activities that may take place in a typical service, and in most instances they will occur in the order given above and will be subtly and inconspicuously manipulated by the male pastor in charge. The various verbal genres with which this study is concerned include greeting, singing, praying, shouting, testifying, and preaching.

The religious language of Pentecostals is an active language, a participatory, experiencing kind of language, and it is a spoken language. In contrast, the religious language examined by theologians and philosophers is more of a contemplative language, descriptive more of intellectual concepts than of experience: "God is omnipotent." "God is three persons." "Heaven is a state of mind." "The devil is real." "There is a hereafter." All of these propositions can be and have been subjects of debate.[7] Religious language or "God-talk," according to William Blackstone, is not "religious language" until it gives rise to "philosophical perplexities."[8] But the study of religious language is not the same as an ethnography of religious speech. Most of the constructs of Pentecostal belief hinge on active verbs that testify to the traditional nature of the transmission of the faith, and most would not easily lend themselves to philosophical debate. The activities inherent in the experience of being Pentecostal nearly always fall into a category that can be described by gerunds, as in the expanded list of verbal genres shown in table 2.

Generic equivalents are possible for some of the active terms frequently used by the Pentecostal community, but many of these are forced or would only appear in the literature *on* Pentecostals; for example, a "shout" (or "shouts") is recognized as a genre for academic study, but the term is not used by the Pentecostals themselves—they would use "shout" only as a verb. Likewise, scholars use terms such as "tongue-speakers" or "the tongues," which simply are not a part of the language of the Pentecostals. Rather, the use of the terms by group members is restricted to the activity as it occurs. Pentecostals would say "she began to speak in tongues" or "she began to speak." Table 2 suggests, too, that once an experience is out of the hands of participants and is "in the hands of God," it ceases to be capable of being categorized—there are no genres on the table that correspond with the activities past "tarrying." It is at this juncture that the experience becomes Pentecostal—that is, the final eight items mark "the Pentecostal experience," the religion in an experiential stage.

Table 2 also traces the activities of the saints and moves toward the conversion experience of the sinner. The first four activities are generally open to full participation by the members of the group, and some, such as singing, may

Table 2. Emic Categories of Pentecostal Religious Speech and Behavior

Pentecostal Term	Participant Name	Genre
singing	singer	song
praying		prayer
witnessing	witness	witness
testifying	testifier (rare)	testimony
preaching	preacher	sermon
healing	healer	(a) healing
baptizing	baptizer (rare)	baptism
shouting		
prophesying	prophesyer (not prophet)	prophecy
interpreting	interpreter	message (interpretation)
tarrying	seeker	
getting a blessing/getting happy		
letting go		
going all the way		
receiving the Holy Ghost/ getting the Holy Ghost		
being filled with the Holy Ghost/receiving the enfilling		
speaking in tongues		
getting saved		

include outsiders. (Many of the songs sung by Pentecostals, however, are choruses they learned as children and are not found in hymnbooks.) Saints are expected to participate fully in all the early activities. If they perform these acts with vigor, the other acts are likely to follow. In fact, performance of the first activities is recognized as preparatory to the final ones. Only saints (and sinners who desire to become group members) participate in the full gamut of acts. The exercise of breaking down an event into its varied components and forcing attention to fine differentiations of message form, content, channel, and key helps in understanding the event as a whole and is the first step toward determining how the components work together to create that coherent whole.

As developed in table 1, "Act Situation" is the equivalent of Hymes's and Richard Bauman's "event," which they have defined as "a culturally defined, bounded segment of the flow of behavior and experience constituting a meaningful context for action."[9] I have also adopted Hymes's use of Gregory Bateson's term "frame" to refer to this bounded segment of behavior.[10] Thus, the first column in table 1 is the frame that encompasses the behaviors delineated in the other columns. The two poles of Table 1 illustrate graphically the difference in perception between an "act" and a "genre." "Acts of speaking" are categories that lie closer to the native context; whereas "preaching" describes a set of speaking behaviors occurring in one frame, the genre "sermon" is recognized by scholars as the verbal product of the "preaching."

Several other aspects of table 1 require explication. Although the category "audience" is included, the table does not indicate what criteria have been used for this column. The explanation is not a simple one. Even though an act may have an indicated audience, it is important to note whether or not the audience is an evaluative one and what form that evaluation takes (see table 3). In his examination of verbal art as performance, Bauman has determined that an evaluative audience is a criterion of performance; there must be an "assumption of responsibility to an audience for a display of communication competence."[11] If we begin with the notion that performance is subject to evaluation by an audience aware of communication competence, it is evident that not all forms of evaluation are as easy to ex-

Table 3. Audience Evaluation of Pentecostal Religious Performance

Frame	Audience	Form of Evaluation
Greeting	Receiver of greeting	Reciprocity based on competence of execution and key
Group singing	Congregation and pastors	Participation based on key verbal praise
Special singing	Congregation and pastors	Applause
Testifying	Congregation and pastors Testimony leader	Formulaic responses and shouting, dancing in spirit
Preaching	Congregation	Formulaic responses
Altar Call	Congregation—saints and "seekers"	Expressive participation, shouts, dancing in spirit

amine as the applause given in response to a "special" song. For example, the simple execution of a greeting ritual, "Praise the Lord," from one group member to another or to a visitor seems not at first to offer any suggestion of audience or evaluation for competence. Yet there are criteria for the proper execution of such a ritual, ground rules that determine how many of the other members one ought to greet, whether hugging or kissing or patting is appropriate for all greeted members, where greeting should take place, and whether greeting may overlap with the first song of the service. The audience in this one-to-one, face-to-face communication is the receiver of the greeting, whose response will depend on two things: the degree of compliance to the ground rules, that is, the competence of execution, and the key in which the greeting is issued. In this case, kinesics and proxemics hold sway over the actual form and content of the message. Reciprocity, then, will follow largely in the same key. The end, or goal, of the greeting is to make a group member or visitor feel welcome and comfortable within the group he or she has just joined. The success of the outcome is determined by the competence of the execution, not just the words spoken. In this case, the art necessarily accompanies the verbal formula. Proper execution is interpreted as an indication of the performer's membership in the established group. The ritual serves to include every person in attendance in the group of the moment.

During the group singing all members are expected to sing loudly and with enthusiasm. The evaluators of how successfully the song has been executed are often the song leader and the pastor, who may chastise the congregation for not singing in a manner proper for the exaltation of the Lord. The singing, then, is a performance meant to communicate the interest, enthusiasm, and sincerity of the congregation. All persons in attendance, of course, form the audience for the performance.

The prayer service is the only segment of the Pentecostal religious service not subject to evaluation by a critical audience. In other Protestant churches, a well-respected member may rise to lead in prayer and deliver an extemporaneous prayer that could be evaluated by the congregation; but Pentecostals all pray individually, aloud. No one prayer can be differentiated from any of the others. Careful attention to tape-recordings of prayer services reveals that some prayers are long, extemporaneous petitions to God, while others may be only slow, moaning formulaic discharges ("Ohhhhh, God," "Thank you, Jesus," "Praise the Lord."). There is no pressure by the pastor for all to pray, or to pray loudly, or even to kneel in a certain manner. Most members kneel at their pews, but others may merely place head in hand or lean with lowered head on the back of the pew in front. Although prayer requests are taken, there is no requirement that individual prayers must include those requests. The prayer service could not, therefore, be considered a performance.

On the other hand, the testifying and the preaching can both be considered verbal communication subject to evaluation by an audience for communication competence, and both can be considered performance. They are, in fact, surprisingly similar in ways that are beneficial for an analysis of women's testimonies. Each is executed by one speaker and evaluated by the audience with verbal responses that indicate audience approval of both the style of execution and the content of the message. Furthermore, a well-executed testimony or sermon may trigger verbal and kinesic behaviors that attest to the successful delivery of a verbal message.

In the case of the altar call, which is the final extension of the sermon, the verbal communication of the sermon proper is abandoned for intense, short promptings intended to create an atmosphere in which participants are able to shed their inhibitions and "let go." The pastor's promptings are accompanied by several important proxemic and kinesic messages that may become more significant than the verbal message. And here the audience evaluation is almost entirely expressed in audience behavior. Verbal evaluations come later in the form of "You should've been here last night. It was really great. Brother Jones had everybody dancing and speaking [in tongues]."

In order to ascertain more clearly the intricacies of a church service at Johnson's Creek, it is necessary to discern which of the acts of speaking are appropriate within which of the structural frames, and what proxemic and kinesic rules accompany them. Table 4 outlines the intersections of the structure of a religious service, differentiating between audience and performance roles. Participants are at once potential performers and audience, switching roles and codes as quickly as they speak or cease to speak; the per-

Table 4. Intersections of a Speech Situation

Performer	Act/Co-occurrence Acts		Audience	Frame
Saint	Greeting Handshakes; hugs		Receiver of Greeting	Greeting ritual
Congregation	Singing Response shouting Waving of hands		Congregation, Pastors Song Leader	Song service
	Praying Shouting Exhortations Speaking in tongues		------- (God)	Prayer service
Testifier	Testifying Storytelling Witnessing Shouting Dancing Speaking in tongues Interpreting Chanting Crying Preaching	Response shouting Speaking in tongues Interpreting Dancing Waving hands Crying	Congregation & Pastors	Testimony service
Singers	Special Singing	Shouting Applause Responsive exhortations	Congregation & Pastors	"Special" song service
Preacher	Preaching Storytelling Witnessing Shouting Dancing Chanting Reading	Response shouting Waving Hands Crying	Congregation	Sermon
Pastor	Call to Altar Healing Shouting Praying Witnessing Pleading Laying on of hands	Speaking in tongues Waving of hands Dancing Chanting Fainting in the spirit Crying Singing Witnessing	Congregation	Altar call

formers become audience, the audience performers. Responses to the speech acts point to the balance that is maintained when one person has the floor or a performance is in progress. Rules of appropriate behavior dictate which acts can overlap, and when they do, one maintains a performer status while others maintain a responding, or audience status.

Table 4 provides insight into the structure of the service and readily displays which of the frames are the most complex. Certainly the most intricately interwoven of the frames are the testimony service and the altar call portion of the sermon proper. The testimony service boasts a testimony leader and a series of star performers who have available to them a long list of verbal performative acts, an avenue for consistent audience response and semi-participation, and the possibility of singing interspersed with the testimonies. No other part of the service balances performer and audience so completely, while clearly maintaining the differentiation between them. Only the second part of the preacher's frame provides a comparable scene—with the preacher maintaining his star performer role and the audience responding en masse. The preacher is no longer performing a sermon in the same sense that he did during the sermon slot; here his rhetoric becomes short, pleading incantations to which the audience responds. The audience is no longer evaluative, either, in the sense that they were during the sermon proper; here, their behavioral participation becomes their evaluation.

The leadership of the pastor at all intersections of the events (frames) that make up the service must be acknowledged and attests to his control over the chain of events, their order and their duration. It is important to note, also, that when the preacher communicates during the sermon, he shares this performance space with no other participant. His is a star performance role; although verbal responses are allowed, the full effect of his speaking must wait to be revealed during the altar call. The evaluation by the audience is their complete involvement in the final scene of the service.

One of the most central concerns of the ethnography of speaking is the description of speech acts, events, and situations. But descriptions are the first step only and must be coupled with the recognition of the cultural system within which the speaking occurs in order, as Bauman and Sherzer put it, to "comprehend the organization of speaking in social life, the relevant aspects of speaking *as* a cultural system." The description of speech occurrence in the Pentecostal religious service given here is an attempt to outline and expose the various verbal genres available to members of the group, the performance aspects of the execution of the verbal art, as well as the perceived goals and outcomes of participation in such activities. However, in an attempt to examine the importance of speech in the Pentecostal community, description must be accompanied by acknowledgment of the importance of the group who practices it: "the point of departure is the speech community, defined in terms of the shared or mutually complementary knowledge and ability (competence) of its members for the production and interpretation of socially appropriate speech."[12]

The Pentecostal community operates on a Bible-inspired hierarchy, based on Paul's letters to the Corinthians, which places women in a position subservient not only to God but to men as well. The speech frames available to women, as well as female manipulation of the various verbal avenues, delineate this hierarchy. Attention to content and style of delivery by men and women of all the verbal genres supports the traditional sex-based roles within the Pentecostal community. This chapter has laid the foundation for further examination of the actual words spoken by the individual participants in the Pentecostal religious service. The following chapter will suggest how women in the Pentecostal group manipulate the forms available to them to maneuver for position within the context of the service and actually acquire temporary control over the event, at the same time establishing group identity and deflecting male dominance and authority.

CHAPTER FOUR

Power of the Word

They'd get up and testify for half an hour. Dance and talk, dance and talk. It just wasn't right. It didn't give the minister a chance to minister them the word. There was three of them. Time they all got done it was time to send everybody home.

BECAUSE of the preponderance of women in Pentecostal services, it might be assumed that women dominate them. They do not. Although women are active participants, male authority and control must not be confused with female spiritual power. For example, although women can be preachers in this faith, they are less often pastors.[1] Men generally maintain the positions of authority in this religion, as is consistent with a biblically-based hierarchy that places women below men. The sex-linked roles in this traditional religious community dictate behavior models and support only those performances that allow for the maintenance and perpetuation of the status quo. Yet, through their expert manipulation of the verbal discourse available to them in the course of a religious service, Pentecostal women do manage to alter the status quo for a short time. This chapter examines Pentecostal women's testimonies—spontaneous, traditional speeches, orally created and performed from the pew during a specifically bounded space of time in the religious service—and shows how these testimonies function for the women who perform them.

In all respects, these spontaneous examples of verbal art can be shown to be traditional. Within the folk group, conceptions of structure, content, and style of delivery are transmitted orally, perceived aurally and duplicated through example. Novices learn by watching and practicing. Young believers are encouraged to testify; their early testimonies expose the most skeletal structural elements of the testimony form. Creative improvisation is developed by the master testifier, but manipulation of the form is always within the elements that can and do tolerate the dynamics of play. Here, as always in folklore genres, there is a working tension between dynamism (change) and conservatism (stability).[2] Experts in the skill of testifying can actually take over the service.

This examination of a specific folkloric genre, religious testimony, is rooted in I.M. Lewis's contention that ecstatic religious traditions are most attractive to those segments of society that are politically impotent, providing them a means for expression and group identity.[3] Discounting any innate tendency toward hysteria in women, Lewis correlates the "peripherality of women" in most, if not all, social systems with female possession tendencies. For women who are largely excluded from participation in the social and political affairs of their world, ecstatic religious experience provides a means of establishing group identity and should be, according to Lewis, recognized as "thinly disguised protest movements directed against the dominant sex." The testimony performances of Pentecostal women illustrate the artful manipulation of performance rules, delivering to the performers and their audience of other women a moment of respite from the domination by the male members of their religious community.

At Johnson's Creek Church, as at other rural Pentecostal churches, women are encouraged to sing loudly, bring special prayer requests to the pastor, testify, sing "specials," listen to the preacher, "let God have his way," and come forward for healing. The entire focus of a service is on the anticipation of the moment(s) when the women are released from their rather formal poses and respond to the ecstatic nature of the service and the admonitions of their male leaders. Women sing, women pray, women testify, women even preach. For all of this activity, however, women manipulate the creative force of their verbal art most obviously in the performance of their testimonies. This can be illustrated by first examining the way Pentecostal women preach and by contrasting their style of preaching with their style of testifying. Although women are allowed to preach, they are not expected to preach "like men"; it is more often in the performance of their testimonies that they are permitted such freedom that they have potential for control of the services.

Pentecostalism permits women to become licensed preachers. One female informant showed me her card as evidence that she was a licensed preacher in the United Apostolic Church of Jesus Christ, Inc. She explained her role as preacher in this way: "I can just do anything my husband can do. Now there are some organizations that don't believe in women ministers. Some won't ordain them, won't give them licenses. But I get my turn, too. I haven't been put down on a regular basis yet, but they've been wanting me to preach a revival." About her style of preaching, she said: "Of course, women, I don't preach like my husband. Everybody has their own style. I would say I preach a lot simpler than my husband does. My husband is just, I'll have to admit it, he's deeper than I am. . . . Now, that's just my style, I mean, I'm just simple. As far as being educated in order to use big words and things like that, Now, my husband can do that." Some of the conflicts surrounding the reality of allowing women to preach are revealed by what this woman says. Even though she has been licensed, she has not been given a regular position for preaching in the church. Furthermore, she is quick to pay deference to her husband as the better preacher and to demean her own capabilities. This woman's statement, as well as subsequent statements by her husband about her, support Robin Lakoff's observation that "we can learn about the way women view themselves and everyone's assumptions about the nature and role of women from the use of language in our culture, that is to say, the language used by and about women."[4] The issue of women preachers in the Pentecostal religion is certainly reflective of the cultural expectations and social role behaviors of both men and women in this faith.

Pentecostal uneasiness about women preachers comes from Biblically supported beliefs about the role and status of women. Since Pentecostals allegedly take the Bible literally, it is even difficult to justify allowing women to speak out in church. Paul wrote to Timothy on this point: "Let the women learn in silence with all subjection. But I suffer not a woman to teach, nor to usurp authority over the man, but to be in silence" (1 Timothy 2:11, 12). And to the Corinthians, Paul wrote: "Let your women keep silence in the churches; for it is not permitted unto them to speak; but they are commanded to be under obedience, as also saith the law. And if they learn anything, let them ask their husbands at home, for it is a shame for women to speak in the church" (1 Cor. 14:34, 35).

The preacher who was frustrated with the women who testified all night and would not allow him time to preach confided how he felt in general about women preachers: "I never did care too much about women preachers. God didn't have any. He told the men to go out and preach the gospel. He never told a woman to do that. Here's what he said, 'A woman's place is at home, rearing the children.' " Primarily, he asserted that women were not equipped to deal with the problems a Pentecostal preacher faces. He related several long, involved stories about how he and other preachers had been forced to fight off persecutors with knives and guns. "Lord told his disciples, 'I send you amongst wolves.' Now, do you think I'd send my wife out amongst a bunch of heathens? Sinners don't care what they do. They'll string you out. They don't care." When asked what the role of women ought to be within the church, he answered: "They are handmaidens. They should wait upon the ministers of the church. A woman's got no right. She is not over a man. A man is over the woman and Christ is over the man, over the church. Now, she's got a place in the church as a Sunday School teacher or maybe as advising to the women. But she can't stand up in that pulpit and tell people what to do because that makes her over the man and that's not according to God's word."

Of course, the central issue here is not the danger involved in the ministry, but the symbolic implications of having a woman stand in the position of authority—behind the pulpit. This clearly makes the men very nervous. That the issue is a sexual one and that women are denied the right to the platform because of their natural role as sexual temptress is supported by the same man's final statement. "A woman can't pull a church together. People won't go to hear a woman preach . . . unless old men *will*. Just to be honest with you, the way a woman might act, squatting around, men *would* go. Some of them old men are just crazy about women preachers."

In contrast, women who feel called to be preachers do find scriptural support for their calling. One female preacher's words are echoed by all women who support female preaching: "The Bible does give us women this right. It says 'in the last days'—this is in Joel and also in Acts—'I will pour out my spirit on all flesh, your sons and your daughters shall prophesy.' And he said, 'Upon my handmaidens I will pour out my spirit.' So the word allows us to be handmaidens and the men have to give us that right." This woman realized that, in contrast to Paul's clear directives that women are not to teach or even to speak, this verse offers a rather weak justification for her own endeavors as a preacher. Most Pentecostals who rely on these verses as proof that women should be able to preach point out that these are the "last days" and that all the preaching possible is needed to save the world before the end comes.

Like the male preacher quoted above, the female preacher is aware of her potential to be viewed as a sex object. She is careful not to present herself as anything other than a meek female who has actually had no choice in the matter.

> I always present myself as a handmaiden of the Lord. Let the men take the part of the ministry and the government of the church because they are the head. The Bible clearly says we are the weaker vessel. Sometimes I'm called to a church and I run into a hard spirit at first. I say, "Relax, I don't call myself a preacher. Let the men do that; it's all right. But you have got to give me the right to be a handmaiden of the Lord and he has poured out his spirit unto me and he has called me into his work and I'm here."

She is acutely aware of the importance of her demeanor and dress while in front of a congregation, and in the following statement this same preacher clearly marks the difference between the way men and women preach.

> I have always tried to be a woman. I resent in my own heart seeing women take the platform and try to be mannish. This is the first mistake women make. We are women. We are the weaker vessel. I try to give honor to the ministry. I try to be subject to them. I never try to act mannish. I don't want to act like a man. I am a woman. I don't exhort and I am not as rambunctious, you might say, as some men. . . . I always dress in white in the platform, because I do not feel that is

> a place to display clothes. Many, many people watch these things.

In the infrequent services where women are allowed to preach, the male pastor of the church leads the service until the woman preacher takes the sermon slot and stands behind the pulpit. When she has finished her sermon, the pastor takes the authority back and conducts the altar call, while the woman returns to her place in the congregation. Lakoff has suggested that "women's language," that is, both language used by women and language about women, "submerged a woman's personal identity, by denying her the means of expressing herself strongly, on the one hand, and encouraging expressions that suggest triviality in subject matter and uncertainty about it, on the other."[5] This is often manifested in speaking of the woman as a sex object and/or by suggesting that she is not a serious person. The following introduction by a male pastor for his preacher wife's sermon is an excellent example of what Lakoff is talking about:

> Sister Connie's going to speak for us tonight. She's been reading and studying and praying all week. I came home, you know, and found a tablet, you know, tablet sheets of paper all over the dresser and so I knew *she'd been up to something*. I finally asked her what it was, and *she admitted* to it and told me a little of it. So, I said, "well, when are you going to do it?" "*Whenever I get the chance*." And I said, "How about this Saturday night." So, I'm glad that she did this, reading and studying the things of God. You know, that's how we grow and I think we ought to be about our father's business. So we're glad to have Sister Connie come. *Glad to have her as a*

> *helpmate.* So I want her to come down and deliver whatever she has. [emphases mine]

Compare the above introduction to another given by the same man when introducing a visiting male preacher: "We're glad to have Brother Richards here with us tonight. We know the Lord has been good tonight, we've really felt the spirit tonight and love to feel the spirit of the Lord. Amen. I know Brother Richards, he's come now a few times to preach for us and I know the way he preaches tonight and I know the rest is going to be full of the same. Amen. We just want him to preach until he gets tired. Everybody that agrees say 'Amen.' "

The pastor-husband's introduction for his wife's "sermon" is a carefully calculated speech meant to place her squarely in her place as trivial woman and his own "helpmate." His description of her activities and what he "found" upon arriving at his home are more suggestive of a parent-child relationship than that of a husband and wife. The full implication is that he "caught" her at something she really ought not to be doing. She "admitted" being "up to something," and will do it whenever he allows her to do it. He never uses the word "preach" in describing what she will do in the pulpit and never suggests that what she will deliver will be inspiring or likely to invoke the spirit of God as he does in introducing the male preacher.

The attitude displayed by this Pentecostal pastor appears to be inconsistent with the commonly held notion that women are more spiritual than men, closer to nature, and more likely to be emotional, be possessed by the spirit, and exhibit uninhibited ecstatic behaviors. The difference is that women are allowed to exhibit all these behaviors only within certain carefully bounded frames of the service. A woman standing behind the pulpit offers such a threat to male authority and control that in that position she is relegated to a narrowly confined role, one that cannot possibly be construed as a "preacher" role. To do so would be to usurp the position of all the men in the room. The female preacher clearly recognizes her precarious position and plays the role of the inadequate woman, sent by God to address the congregation. She is careful to reassure everyone in attendance that she will comply with all their expectations; she will play the game with the prescribed rules. Sister Connie begins her sermon this way.

> Well, I kinda hope you all aren't expecting too much. He kinda put me out there on a limb. I praise the Lord tonight because truly he is so good to me. . . . Now, I want you to know that I never thought about these things on my own. I prayed and the Lord revealed these things to me. I have not got that much sense in my own head. The Lord has to show me these things. I'm not intelligent. I never went to college. I don't have any education, learning in this world. But whatever the Lord give me he give it to me straight from him. . . . We'll start. Now this may be kinda like teaching, I don't know, you know, sometimes it's kinda hard to preach, but maybe a mixture of both, preaching and teaching.

Testifying, on the other hand, is available as a verbal genre to both sexes of the congregation. While all members are expected to deliver their witness for the Lord as often as possible, in reality more women testify than do men and more women than men testify on a regular basis. A typical testimony might take the form of the following, delivered on May 24, 1980, by an unidentified man who was visiting Johnson's Creek Church: "I'm glad I know the Lord. It's been about fifty-seven years ago. I was going blind and I got baptized in Jesus'name. The power of God came down and healed my body, filled me with his spirit. I'm thankful tonight to know that he'll answer prayers, anything that you have need of." Such a testimony can be heard at nearly any Pentecostal church service. It is a standard testimony capable of being delivered in any setting. This man was a visitor to Johnson's Creek; although he was not a part of that church community, his testimony was recognized by the group as satisfactory. The same general type of testimony will often be heard in revivals or camp meetings that draw from several church communities. Most Pentecostals would, in fact, define a testimony as a speech that asserts something particular that God has done for the speaker. The concept of testifying is closely aligned with the notion of "witnessing." Through witnessing members encourage outsiders to come to church or seek the Holy Ghost by telling them stories about their own conversions and the miraculous things God has done for them since.

Within the context of the closely knit church community at Johnson's Creek, the idealized notion of what constitutes a testimony, and what, in fact, the women say when they testify are often two different things. Analysis of many testimonies delivered in the context of this one church community reveals patterns of speaking, patterns of delivery, and a consistency of content that is quite unlike the man's testimony given above. Seldom do the women at Johnson's Creek testify about what God has done for them in terms of a specific healing or a deliverance from danger or pain. Theirs is a shared testimony that confirms their role and status in the community and in their homes and calls on the other women for support to enable them to continue in those roles. At the same time, testifying provides a forum for creative speaking and a temporary lapse of the normal social impotency of the women. Each woman at Johnson's Creek can create for herself a space as the center of attention, and, if her delivery is convincing and effective, she may, in fact, take control of the situation, causing things to happen, altering the social situation, inverting the status quo, but only for the allotted time. As the testifier she does not take over the platform of authority; from her position within the congregation, she reaffirms her position and confirms everyone's expectations. Yet, she manages to manipulate the situation to her advantage, seeking an emotional and creative outlet while communicating her concerns to her sisters, asking for their unabated support for her efforts to sustain her role.

In describing the Mexican corrido as a performance event, John McDowell draws on Roger Abrahams's use of the term "enactment."[6] The same approach will aid in conceptualizing the testimonies performed in the context of a church service at Johnson's Creek. Abrahams has defined "enactment" as "a cultural event in which community members come together to participate, employ the deepest and most complex multivocal and polyvalent signs and symbols of their repertoire of expression, thus entering into a potentially significant experience." Like the corridos, the testimonies embody a "powerful statement of community values and orientations." In order to show how this is so, I will examine testimonies of the women at Johnson's Creek, to illustrate how structurally, thematically, and stylistically these testimonies comment upon community values and expectations and how in their performed context they become and elicit "significant experiences."

The testimonies of the Johnson's Creek women are highly formulaic. They display standard beginnings and endings; enough formulaic statements are available for a testifier to give an entirely appropriate testimony without injecting a single novel phrase into the delivery. Testimonies may exhibit personal creativity in either content or style of delivery, if the structure of the testimony is maintained. Table 5 indicates the various traditional phrases that occur and recur in the testimonies at Johnson's Creek. The following

Table 5. Formulaic Phrases Occurring in Testimonies

I want to thank the Lord	
	for the privilege of being in his house tonight
	for the privilege of standing before him
	for the privilege of testifying here tonight
Tonight before I came I felt so bad, so tired and worn out	
	but now I'm glad I'm here.
I know he is real.	
I want to praise him tonight	for all the things he's done for me
	for his spirit.
I love him tonight.	
I know he is able to do all things.	
He's a great big God.	
It's my desire (my heart's desire)	to be stronger.
	to walk closer to him.
	to stand by him.
	to be in heaven with him.
I want to receive his blessing	tonight.
	to help me through the week.
I desire your prayers.	
Pray for me that I will	do what he'd have me do.
	do what he'd want me to do.
	do his will.
	grow closer to him.
I don't want to be lost.	
I don't know what tomorrow (next week) will bring.	

Table 5, *Continued*

He won't pull me down.
fail me.

He will put his arms close around me.
is a mighty friend.
will stand close beside me.
will keep his hand upon me.
No matter what happens.

I want to be ready to meet him.

Without Jesus I am nothing.
there is no heaven.

I want to go all the way with him.
to let him have his way.

Let go.

Get more.

Reach out.

Obey.

Praise the Lord.

Thank you Jesus.

Hallelujah

Truly tonight. . .

actual testimonies illustrate how these standard, formulaic lines are rendered in performances in the church context. I have rendered my transcriptions of testimonies into lines to indicate where natural and dramatic breath pauses occur during actual performances.[7]

TESTIMONY 1

I'm so glad to be here, tonight.
I'm glad for Jesus.
For his many blessings.
I praise him tonight
Because he's kept his hands upon us
During this hot weather.
No doubt there's many people
Left this earth
Because of the heat.
I'm thankful tonight that Jesus
Showed his mercy toward us
I love him tonight.
And I have a desire
to go all the way with him.

TESTIMONY 2

Tonight I want to thank the Lord
for the privilege of being in his house.
I told my children tonight
I felt so bad,
But once I got here I felt better.
Praise the Lord.
I'm glad to be here tonight.
I know he's real.
I praise him tonight
Because I can be out to the house of the Lord.
He is able tonight to do all things.
I love him tonight.
I praise him for everything.

Tonight it's my desire to be stronger
and grow closer to him.
I desire your prayers
So I can get his favors,
Do what he'd have me to do.

TESTIMONY 3

I want to thank the Lord tonight
For what he means to me.
I want to thank him
Because I know that he's a great big God
And is here to take me through
If I will just put my hand in his.

The three testimonies given here are obviously based almost entirely upon identifiable formulaic phrases and stanzas as illustrated in table 5. As simple examples of actual testimonies, they can serve to illustrate certain structural "positions" within the testimonies (see table 6). The first position is the introduction. Introductory formulas are fairly standard and generally fall into what I shall designate as Position 1; some of the phrases characteristic of the introduction, however, may appear also in the body of a testimony as fillers or stalls. Position 1 usually takes a variation of the following form and carries what Roman Jakobson has designated an "emotive function," serving as it does to focus on the speaker's "attitude toward what he is speaking about."[9]

P1 *I want to thank the Lord tonight*
For the privilege of being in his house tonight.
[or]
I'm glad to be here tonight.
[or]
I want to stand up tonight and praise the Lord
For letting me be here tonight.

Table 6. Structural Framework of Testimonies at Johnson's Creek Church

Position 1:	Introduction Formulaic Phrases
Position 2:	Metanarrational devices or personal note, to introduce the—
Position 3:	Narration or personal experience stories
Position 4:	Explication (narrational message)
Position 5:	Closing

Other narratives or explication can appear between Positions 1 and 5:

Position 2_2:	Second metanarrational device to introduce the—
Position 3_2:	Second narration or personal experience stories
Position 4_2:	Explication

or, testimonies may simply insert several examples of position 4 in sequence, as in Testimony 4 above.

The standardized, identifiable introduction may actually contain two or more parts, the second serving to reiterate the first. When positions are further segmented into identifiable subgroupings, I have designated these with a subscript number, $P1_1$. For example:

$P1_1$ *I told my children tonight*
I felt so bad,
But once I got here I felt better.
[or]
There are a lot of things
I could be doing tonight.
And I'd probably enjoy a few of them.
But you know I enjoy coming to church.

Position 2, which serves to direct the focus from the addresser to the addressee, generally takes the form of a metanarrational device intended to introduce an upcoming narrative, and serves a vocative or imperative function that instructs the addressee to "listen," as well as doubly serving a phatic or contact function intended to establish and maintain communication.[10] We use metanarrational devices in both formal and informal speech to signal the listener: "Let me tell you a story about that" or "that happened to me once."

In the most variable position in a testimony, Position 3, a performer may employ a narrational mode of discourse. Forms of narration range from complete stories to reminiscences to fragmented narratives. Many of the stories embedded within testimonies given by women at Johnson's Creek take the form of exempla, or stories told with the intent to convey a moral or spiritual message. I have designated the explication of these stories within the testimonies as Position 4. The explication serves to justify the relating of the narrative within the context of the testimony and the religious service; it also serves to mark the end of one narration. Testimonies may, in fact, relate several reminiscences, personal experience stories, or anecdotes. The transition from one to another is generally recognized by the framing that the metanarrational device (Position 2) and the explication (Position 4) provide.

The following testimony is representative of the women's testimonies at Johnson's Creek. Note the use of formulaic phrases within easily discernible positions. The performer's use of the narrative mode appears in two separate personal experience stories and reminiscences (Position 3).

TESTIMONY 4

P1. *I wouldn't want to come out to the*
House of the Lord
Without testifying
You know, I love the Lord with all my heart
And I want to walk close to him
Because I realize like Martha said
It's going to take a holy life,

A pure clean life
And you got to have it down deep in our souls
If we're going to make it through,
Because we're not going to fool God anytime.
He knows everything we do tonight
And everything we say
And if we're not true to him
He knows all about it.
You know I want to walk close to him.
$P2_1$ *I want to tell you about it.*
You know, we sing that song about "Honey in the Rock."
You know, I love that song.
$P3_1$ *But years and years and years ago*
When I was a little girl,
We still sung that "Honey in the Rock."
It was still just the same.
We can go to the Lord and the rock and
The foundation
And they say it tastes sweet and it tastes good.
There's Honey in the rock.
You know, people that don't realize that
God's word says these things,
Unless you understand what's it's talking about
You won't understand what you're saying.
Back then, when I was a child,
We'd play back of the church.
We'd get together as children and do the singing
And pray, of course, we was
Trying to—we wasn't trying to make fun—
We was trying to follow what the old folks did.
And I had a cousin,
She had to sing "Honey in the Rock"
Every time we "had church."
I sang that song so much
I got tired of singing that song,
But she wouldn't have church if she didn't sing
"Honey in the Rock" first.
But, you know, I love that song

But back then I just didn't want to sing that song at all
Because I got so tired of it.
But I didn't realize what we was a singing about.
It was just so much singing,
It was just words.
In other words, to get the meaning out of it.
It wasn't seeing how good God was and how good the song was.
I don't know why she loved it so good,
But she always wanted to sing it.
But I'll always think about it.
It's been many, many years,
Still every time we sing that song,
I think of her.
Now, since I know what I'm singing about,
I really love to sing that song.
And truly I love the Lord.

$P2_2$ *And I think about so many times*
So many times when we
When things that have happened many years ago,
Things come up like this.
They still bring memories back to you.

$P3_2$ *The old times when we used to have such good services,*
So many people would come out.
Of course, there wasn't nothing else to go to
Only church, back then.
There wasn't nothing around in the country here
Of the world to go to
And we didn't have no cars
And no way of going anywhere
Only walk and go in the horse and buggy
Or horses and wagons
And everybody almost that was able went to church,
Sinners and everybody and the house would be full
And outside the yard would be full
Standing around.
And so many children, ah, yes,

And so many of them have gone on to meet the Lord
And so many of them were faithful to God all these years
And all the goodness of the earth.
Thinking about it so many times

P4 *You know, the good things of God,*
How good he's been to us
And how he's kept us all these years
Brought us through so many hard places
So many heartaches and so many trials
So many tests that God has put us, brought us through.
He's always brought us out victorious.

P5 *Truly tonight, I love him with all my heart.*
I want to walk closer to him
And do the things that he'd be pleased with
And do just what he'd have me to do.
Pray for me.

The first eleven lines of this testimony illustrate the creative manipulation of standard formulaic lines rendered by a seasoned testifier, especially in her multifaceted introduction (Position 1). In the body of her testimony this performer inserts two personal experience narratives introduced by standard metanarrational devices that alert the listener to the impending story. Position 2_1 (metanarrational device) in the first half of the testimony takes the form of: "I want to tell you about it." The story proper, Position 3, begins: "But years and years and years ago, when I was a little girl." Position 3_2 designates the second metanarrational device in this testimony, which introduces a narrative closer in style to a reminiscence: "And I think about so many times . . . things come up like this. They still bring back memories to you." In the first narrative, the testifier tells about a young cousin who would not play church without first singing "Honey in the Rock." In order to justify telling that story in the church context, the performer clearly intends the story to contain a message for the group. This is made clear in the explication of her story (Position 4): "But back then I just didn't realize what we was a singing about . . . people don't realize. Unless you understand what it's talking about, you won't understand what you're saying." Her story is meant to direct church members to pay attention to what they are singing about in order to understand the song's meaning. Structurally, the lines further serve to signal the end of the narrative. This patterning follows the text-context-application pattern of Puritan sermons that Rosenberg documents as appearing in contemporary folk sermons.[11] Her first personal experience narrative leads her naturally into reminiscing about what going to church used to be like (Position 3_2): "They still bring memories back to you," which introduces another narrative that is, in turn, followed by its own explication (Position 4).

Position 5, or the closing, is usually as standard and formulaic as Position 1, the introduction. In the testimony above it is clear to the listener when the performer is "winding down" and the testifier relies more completely on formulas. Both the formulaic paterns of these lines and the delivery style serve to signal the termination of the testimony.

TESTIMONY 5

P1 *Hallelujah, thank you, Lord, Hallelujah,*
The Lord is wonderful tonight.
P2 *I'm going to tell this little old story*
For the benefit of those who need a blessing.
P3 *You know, I had a window in the kitchen that was broke out.*
So, Brother Willie put a piece of tin in there.
And he had a little hole in there,
He was going to put a stove in there,
But that didn't work out too good.

But he left the tin there and, you know,
That just bothered me and bothered me and bothered me
And I wanted that tin out of there so bad.
But I couldn't find any glass to put in it,
So finally it bothered me so much that I got up
And I went through all the junk and everything around
And I hunted for some glass until I fixed it.

P4 *You know what? It's so much better to*
Have light than it is to have darkness.
It's so much better to have Jesus living within you
Than to have these old burdens deep down in here
Just pressing down, you know.
And you know what?
It was worth every minute of the effort I put forth
To get that glass in there.
Tonight, I want you to reach up to Jesus.
Oh, Hallulujah, I believe he's worth every effort
That we put forth.
The things that he can give us
Can take us through another week
Another month.
Whatever we need.
The Lord will be there
To give it to us.

P5 *I desire your prayers.*
I love the Lord tonight
And I know he's an answering God.

Note that the most popular connectors in the testimonies of the women at Johnson's Creek are "you know" and "tonight"; these are used consistently and provide continuity from testimony to testimony. The "you know" serves a stylistic function as well, maintaining the phatic (contact) function of communication. The "tonight" serves to place the testimony in the immediate context, attempting, actually, to destandardize the testimony, but in the process becoming one of the most standard features of the deliveries.

Women at Johnson's Creek deliver their testimonies in a wide range of styles. A woman may stand abruptly, deliver a standardized, completely formulaic testimony, and sit down. In general, women who perform in this manner do so consistently. On the other hand, other women in the group become recognized as the performers of creative, personalized testimonies, while still others may rely on standard formulas but expend their creative energies on the style of delivery rather than content. From service to service, the individual testifiers have identifiable styles of testimony delivery.

It is a sacred duty to give a testimony, to witness as often as possible to the glory of the Lord. The women at Johnson's Creek Church take this obligation seriously and most deliver a testimony at each service they attend. While a hastily delivered formulaic testimony fulfills the requirement to testify, there is no question but that the most important aspect of a woman's testimony performance is its effect on the audience. In fact, audience reaction to a testimony, like audience reaction to a folk sermon, is the manifestation of the audience evaluation of the competency of the performer. Testimonies delivered in a rushed, self-conscious manner rarely merit more that a quiet "Amen" at their termination. The women who deliver them are not capitalizing on the potential for power that lies with an effective delivery; they are merely meeting the obligation to give testimony. Effective delivery may rely on structure, style of delivery, content, or combinations thereof. The following is a transcription of a testimony that relies almost entirely upon formulaic stanzas delivered one after another. The transcription may suggest a rather staid testimony, as the performer does not allow herself to interject personal statements nor does she use a narrative in her testimony. But this performer has a unique testimony delivery style. Her performances are always long and seem to ramble, but her style of delivery is sincere, tearful, high-pitched, fast, nearly breathless, and very close to a chant, complete with the gasp at the end of the line.

TESTIMONY 6

P1 *I praise the Lord tonight*
For what he is to me and for another privilege
Of being in the house of God,
Because he's kept us safe for yet another day.
If you love the Lord
You wouldn't want to do anything
To disgrace his name, uh.
I've found him a true friend
In time of trouble.
You know God is always near
If we just call upon him, uh,
There's so many times
We grumble and complain
And we don't always understand
The things that God's taking us through, uh,
But then someone will come along
And will say something
That will touch our hearts
And bring us back
Into the avenues of truth, uh,
You know God is always there.
I was sitting there thinking
About that song that said
"Just go and tell Jesus on me," uh,
"Whatever our weakness may be," uh,
"If you are my brother,
Then don't tell another,
Just go and tell Jesus on me," uh.
You know, sometimes
We go to others with our trials and our tasks

And the things that are brought our way
And talk about one another
In ways that are not Christian-like.
P2 *This was brought home so forcefully*
P3 *The other day when Lana came home*
And she said when she got in trouble
She just went to God with it,
P4 *You know, and I thought, my,*
How much better our lives would be
If we'd all follow that policy.
When we're in trouble
And we see our loved ones in trouble
If we'd just go to God
He has the answer to every problem.
P5 *Pray for me*
That I may walk the straight and narrow way.

The introduction to this testimony is standard (lines 1-4) and is followed by a series of formulaic subparts strung together, an aborted narrative, and a standard, formulaic conclusion. However, it is the style of delivery of this testimony that will concern us here.

The introduction was delivered in a low-key tone in recitation style. However, by the fifth, sixth, and seventh lines, the delivery had accelerated considerably, the pitch of the voice had risen, and the delivery became akin to the folk preacher's style with an "uh" punctuating the ends of lines 7, 11, 15, 20, 24, 25, and 28. As might be expected, the most personal lines in this testimony, lines 34-37, deviate from the chanted style, but they were, nevertheless, delivered in a high-pitched, breathless manner. This testimony was delivered in the same service as Testimony 5 given above. Although radically different in structural composition, both testimonies elicited intense audience response as a result of their deliveries.

The following is another testimony by the same woman

who delivered Testimony 5 above; both are typical testimony performances for this woman. It is common for her to be enthusiastic in her performance; she frequently uses narrative and interjects personal elements into her testimonies. She is extremely adept at gaining empathy with her audience by relying on phatic questions such as "and you know what?" and "you know what I mean"?; she makes direct pleas to her audience, too, such as "I want you to reach up to Jesus." It is important to note that this is the same woman who was allowed to preach on the night described above.

TESTIMONY 7

Blessed Jesus. Thank you Jesus.
Tonight I love the Lord.
I thank him tonight
And I praise him
Because I know he's real in my heart
This night.
As we sang that song "Jesus on the mainline"
It just made me think you know
When you dig around sometimes
You get down there
And you get these little streams.
You know, these little streams
They're just not enough,
There's just not enough water there.
But when we hit that main line,
Hallelujah,
You've got plenty of water,
You've got plenty,
When you get Jesus on the main line.
Hallelujah.
You've got just what you need.
You know, those little trinkles
They don't do much for me,
Thank you Jesus,

For I've been under the Holy Spout.
Hallelujah.
It does a whole lot more for me,
Thank you Jesus.
Halleujah.
You know I might make you stay up for a while
Because, praise the Lord,
Hallelujah,
I know *he is real!*
Whoooooooo!
Glory!
I know he is real tonight.
You know when I sing
And when I testify
Everybody looks at me
And they think I'm kind of
Peculiar.
But you know tonight
We are peculiar people.
But you know something?
I'm not ashamed of Jesus
Hallelujah.
Because this is the Lord
That I sing
That I testify for
That I stomp my feet for
That I clap my hands for
It's Jesus Christ
And I love him tonight,
Lord,
And he is worthy
Of all praises,
Everything,
Everything
That we can possible do for him
He is worthy of it
This night.
Hallelujah!
Whoooooooooooooo

This woman's performance of a testimony is actually much closer to a general preaching style than is her preaching; furthermore, in many ways, this particular testimony is much closer to a sermon than it is to a testimony. Like the folk sermons discussed by Rosenberg, this woman's testimony suggests a smoothness of content and delivery that might only come through repeated performances, even though the testifier, like the folk preacher, would insist that testimonies are a gift of the Holy Ghost and are spontaneously inspired by God.[12] The notion of a prepared testimony would be just as abhorrent to the testifier as the memorized or practiced sermon would be to a folk preacher. The themes elaborated by the female testifier are more comparable to those that might be used by the preacher than to the usual content of testimonies. This testifier is able to leave the text-context-application rigidity and spontaneously create a "sermon" built on the images of trickles, streams, and the Holy Spout. As with sermons, single lines or thoughts are expanded, but the reliance on narrative themes can be bypassed if just enough logic holds the sermon together.

In the mode of the sermons, this testimony is chanted (although she is at all times intelligible) and the delivery of individual lines is quite metrical:

Because this is the Lord
That I sing
That I testify for
That I stomp my feet for
That I clap my hands for

As with the other testimonies, this performance has been transcribed to indicate the testifier's own breath punctuation. Notice that this testimony has shorter lines, indicative of a chanted delivery. The delivery style would signify to the group that the woman was filled with the spirit during this testimony, as the folk preacher is "fed by God."[13] Meter, rhyme, rhythm, and timing are all in evidence in this testimony performance.

Both of the testimonies of this woman transcribed here emulate preaching styles set firmly within a testimony frame, especially through the use of introductions that mark them as testimony, and by the delivery from a pew in the congregation. But the preaching style of delivery as well as the audience response and enthusiastic reaction to these testimonies suggest the capacity of the testifying to serve the same function as preaching. In fact, in the testimony given above, the performer is unable to use a standardized, formulaic closing because of the overwhelming emotional response of the audience. The significant point is, of course, that women can speak like preachers within the framework of a testimony, but they cannot do so within the frame of the sermon. It is interesting to note as well that when this same woman was at the pulpit, she set her "preaching" within an identifiable testimony frame by inserting the following formula into the first part of her sermon: "I praise the Lord tonight / Because truly he is so good to me." This may have been an attempt on her part to assure her male counterparts that she knows her place even though she is, at the moment, in a man's place in the pulpit.

Testimony 7 supports the contention that this artful performer knows the potential for control of the service through her verbal skills. This testimony was delivered rapidly and was close in style to a preacher's chant. By the time the woman had finished her performance, the entire congregation of women was marching around the church, dancing and swooning "in the spirit." The audience response to her testimony was unanimous. The performer gained complete control of the situation as she and the other members, mostly women, began to "feel something" and identified it as God in the room. The shouting in response to this testimony lasted a full nine and a half minutes. The entire group became one in its complete surrender to the ecstatic experience; it is at such times that tongue-speaking is likely to appear within the testimony service and did occur immediately following the testimony. Throughout the shouting period, the testifying woman could be heard speaking in tongues. At seven and a half minutes into the shouting time, she was permitted to dominate the floor again and speak loudly in tongues. She then interpreted her own tongue speaking.

Not only is the testimony discussed above poetic and the delivery powerful, the content of the message is loaded with importance for the performer and her audience. The esoteric message gives her words their impetus: we are peculiar, and we're not ashamed of it. She outlines what behavior will prove the women's pride in themselves and in their religion: singing, testifying, stomping, clapping. The response to this testimony attests to its success as a performance. The content of the testimony reflects and reinforces the shared beliefs, attitudes, and values of the women. Delivery style and content work together to lend emotional power to the performance. All the testimonies in a given testimony service contribute to the creation of a complex entity, a rich mixture of communal knowledge, signs, and symbols interplayed against a backdrop of religious significance.

The testimonies of the women at Johnson's Creek reflect a deep sense of the women's own place in a cultural scheme that positions them under the men in their lives and subjects them to the will and domination of all men as well as the will and domination of their male religious figure, Jesus Christ. According to their world view, their place is in the home and in the church. If a meeting is scheduled, it is their duty to be there. The frequent apology for wanting to stay at home instead of coming to church is a confession of weakness and is a submission to the demands of God to be "in his house." The assertion that God's house is where a woman wants to be, and that now that she's here she's so glad she came are gestures of appeasment to a potentially angry God. She nearly always thanks God, in fact, for the "privilege" of being in his house, thanks him for allowing her the physical ability to come. Her presence is a tribute to his benevolence.

The formulaic phrases in the testimonies of these women reflect a remarkably low self-esteem. They perceive themselves as weak, failing God, doubting, and not following his directives. Openly, publicly, the women profess the desire to "be stronger, walk closer, stand by him, do his will, do what he wants" in order that Jesus will not "fail me," or "pull me down," but will keep his "arms around me, be a mighty friend, stand close, keep his hand on me." The general tone in the testimonies is fatalism; the only hope for dealing with a bleak unknown is to believe that there is a cause/effect factor existing between their compliance to the wishes of an unseen God and his protection from hardship and pain. Many of the testimonies attest to the "trials and tasks of life," the "cross of life," the "burden that we have to bear," the expectation that "next week is going to be tough," and that "life is full of problems and troubles." But the testimonies also reflect the hope for something better. Here on earth, life becomes bearable because Jesus will be a friend and protect the believer if she obeys his every demand, and heaven is the promise of the ultimate "better place," also available only to those who "walk the straight and narrow path." By and large, the testimonies serve to let the women speak to one another about how difficult their plight in life is, how they are attempting to cope, and to request that their sisters pray for their ability to continue to do what is expected of them.

Like the folk preacher, the testifier relies on her skill in manipulating and recreating formulas as well as on her knowledge of and sensitivity to the powerful emotional effect of theme and content on her audience. When she gains control over the situation, structure, style, and theme are intertwined to create the "significant experience"—the enactment of the testimony. The women identify this moment as the experience of a "blessing"; any or all of them may leave the testimony frame and begin to shout, dance, cry, march, and speak in tongues. The blessing that is associated in the women's minds with a shouting, uninhibited service is the assurance from God that he is real, that there is hope for next week, and no matter what happens he will be there to help them—if they are good Pentecostal women. The reaffirmation of God as real and as present in the room is complete with the tongue-speaking and the interpretation of what God "said" through the tongue speaker. The tongues themselves are a sign to the group that God is present and has shown himself through the speech of a woman. The interpretation of the tongues given in the above service is closely aligned with the tenor of the testimonies and serves to answer the requests of the women that God will not fail them, will not forsake them, will keep them safe. The lines come from the Bible and are given as the words spoken by God to Joshua following the death of Moses: "As I was with Moses, so I will be with thee. I will not fail thee, nor forsake thee" (Joshua 1:5).

When the testimony enactment occurs, the performer and the members of her community become one, in sentiment and in purpose. For a brief time in most Pentecostal testimony services, the power of the speaking women threatens male authority. Of course, it never gets out of hand; the authority of the male pastor to reestablish the structural components of the service is not lost, only obscured. But it is precisely at the moment of communal "blessing" that the women create a situation in which they exhibit their own natural powers, a space in which to be free to communicate with each other and experience in that moment ecstatic joy. And as long as the moment is recognized by the group as the manifestation of God's spirit, rather than the women's spirit, their moment is secure.

Women have developed a forum for a traditional expressive verbal art within the Pentecostal religious service. That forum is not, however, easily discernible or readily extrapolated from the service as a whole. Women can preach, but the restrictions upon their verbal and kinesic behaviors in a position behind the pulpit are constricting and serve to diminish their effectiveness in that position. From her pew, however, the Pentecostal woman can stand and speak; from that position she and the members of her sister group are able to transform the service through their verbal powers. They gain control through verbal art—short-lived control, to be sure, but a masterful illustration of the power of words.

Conclusion

> *It's just something to enrich your life. I can't, well, when I see somebody that just never goes to church, I think, well, they have to have something else to fulfill it, I guess. And me, I don't know of anything else that I could get to fulfill my life, fill that spot, I mean I don't do anything else. But I would hate awful bad for something to happen to this little church up here. I don't know what I'd do really.*

WHEN I first began doing fieldwork in the Pentecostal churches of southern Indiana, I thought perhaps I had stumbled upon a truly egalitarian American situation where women were free to participate openly in religious church services alongside their men. But long months of continued fieldwork and diligent examination of the history of this charismatic religion brought me to an opposite conclusion: the Pentecostal church is one of the best evidences of male dominance and female submission in a modern American context. With the writing of this book, I feel I have settled into some sensible middle ground between these two extreme views. The Pentecostal religion is egalitarian in its belief that all "saints," both male and female, have the right and even the obligation to openly express their joyful worship of God. This belief is responsible for the Pentecostal assertion that both men and women can be preachers. But the belief and the practice diverge rather dramatically at the point of actual implementation: women can be preachers, yes, but at the same time they must be careful not to emulate men or threaten male authority. The belief that men have been placed above women in a heaven-inspired hierarchy is more firmly entrenched than the belief that anyone can be a preacher. Being able to interpret what I was observing in the Pentecostal churches took careful fieldwork combined with research into the history and belief system of this twentieth-century phenomenon.

The focus for this study seemed, then, to pivot around certain new questions: What are the limits of women's expressive behavior in the Pentecostal religious service? How is that expressive behavior modulated? What are the benefits to women who participate in this charismatic religion?

In order to answer these questions it became necessary to trace the participation of women in the Pentecostal religion, to read scholarly examinations of female participation in ecstatic religions, to explore the church community, to reconstruct the male and female roles within the religion, and to construct an ethnography of general communication within the Pentecostal religious service before I could extract from that complete picture the specifics of communicative expression available to women, how they manipulate those communicative forms, and what the rewards are for their active participation.

The Pentecostal folk community is a male-centered hierarchy that places God at the top, followed by Jesus Christ, followed by men, followed by women, followed by children. The Pentecostal religious service is male dominated and male manipulated. Yet women can and do participate freely and openly in carefully regulated segments of the religious services. Their active participation and the exhibition of their spiritual powers are desired because there is a generally held belief that women are naturally able to conjure spirits and commune with God. All Pentecostals, both male and female, long for the moment in the service when all propriety can be abandoned and persons are set free to express themselves in an uninhibited manner. This moment of freedom is largely created by the women and is, to be sure, coveted by the women. But the significance of the well-executed testimony performance goes far beyond personal release of inhibition. The performance of the testimony provides the female performer a modicum of control over the other participants in the religious service. If performed well, the testimony can serve as catalyst for general church-wide response; the female performer who recognizes her own potential for power can pursue the control she knows is possible. The Pentecostal sociocultural situation is so constrictive on female members that any promise of control and power in the service situation holds weight far beyond its desert. Yet, recognition of the magnitude of importance the scene takes on for the women who learn to manipulate it leads us closer to an understanding of the importance of the religion in the lives of its female adherents as well as a better understanding of the lure of the sect for females in general.

This study has provided evidence for several contentions: 1) it is important to study individual religious communities and focus on the beliefs and behaviors of a single representative example of a much larger, wide-spread phenomenon; 2) it is necessary to recognize the sociocultural matrix within which expressive behaviors and cultural performances occur; 3) the study of verbal art in performance can only be undertaken with verbatim transcripts of performances in hand; and 4) basing the study of female behavior ipso facto upon ancient or ill-founded folk beliefs gets us no closer to understanding what is, in fact, occurring in modern American Pentecostal churches. When our study begins with these several premises in mind, subsequent research in American folk religion will, indeed, add to our general knowledge and understanding of religious women and men as well as our understanding of women and men in general.

APPENDIX

A Testimony Service

THE TESTIMONY SERVICE

One testimony does not usually, by itself, act as a catalyst for spontaneous responses from the group. The context for uninhibited behaviors, shouting, dancing, and speaking in tongues is created by the testimony service as a whole. In order to illustrate how the testimonies build on one another and how one performance influences another, I shall present the entire testimony service from Johnson's Creek which occurred on Saturday night, May 17, 1980. The service began with two songs and group prayer. The transcription begins with the first testimony of the testimony service. The pastor was serving as testimony leader. Congregational responses are on the right; explanatory notes are in brackets.

TESTIMONY 1

Tonight I want to thank the Lord for the privilege	
Of being in his house.	
I told my children tonight I feel so bad,	
But once I got here I felt better	Yes, Lord
Praise the Lord.	Oh, Thank you, Jesus
I'm glad to be here tonight.	
I feel him in my soul.	

You know, God is real. Thank you, Jesus
I praise him tonight Hallelujah!
Because I am able to be in the house of the Lord, uh,
He is able tonight to do all things.
I love him tonight.
I praise him for everything. OHHH, thank you, Jesus
Tonight it's my desire to be stronger
And grow closer to him. Yes, Lord
I desire your prayers so I can get in
And serve the Lord
Do what he'd have me to do Yes, Lord
Seems like I can't sing or talk either one Oh, Lord
But I know God's able to make a way—yes Yes, Lord
[Final line is lost in group response.] Hallelujah, Yes,
Lord, OHHHHHHH, Lord
Amen, Lord, Hallelujah!!
Oh, Lord

TESTIMONY 2

I want to thank the lord for his many blessings
Tonight
And for taking care of us.
[Line inaudible, voice low.]
I don't want to be lost. Oh, Jesus, help her, Lord
There are a lot of things I could be doing tonight
And I'd probably enjoy a few of them.
But you know I enjoy coming to church Yes, Lord
WHOOOOOOOOO!
I enjoy coming and receiving a blessing from God.
Because I know that that blessing
I receive tonight
Will be what will pull me through this next week.
I don't know how many days the Lord
Might let me be here next week,
Maybe the whole week.
I know he's never going to try me Yes, Lord, hallelujah
Or try to pull me down Oh, Jesus

He's going to work with me
And he's going to put his arms close around me—
Thank you, Jesus
But I know tonight that my blessings tonight
Are going to pull me through next week
Yes, Lord
Amen, Lord, yes, Lord
Hallelujah, Lord, amen
WHOOOOOOOOOO! Lord, thank you, Jesus

I'm going to be safe Thank you, Lord
I know because the Bible says
"Eye has not seen, neither has the ear heard,
The things God has prepared for them
That love Him."
You know we can't even begin to imagine Heaven.
Oh, we talk about heaven
And we talk about those beautiful streets,
And, oh, my goodness Oh, thank you, Jesus
Oh, we talk about them
But we can't even begin to imagine Praise God
Our minds are so small.
We can't even imagine such beauty. Thank you, Jesus
And tonight I want to go there and see it.
I want to spend all eternity
Just roaming around through heaven
OHHHHHHHHHH, Jesus
One place after another Thank you, Sweet Jesus
And just see what it's all about
And what it's all like Thank you, Jesus
Truly tonight I do love the Lord so much
And I do want to go all the way with him.
Amen, hallelujah
Jesus, Jesus, OHHHHHHHH

TESTIMONY 3

You know, truly tonight I want to thank God
For all that he's done for me Yes, Lord

And I been asking for prayer for this girl at work
And tonight right before we got off from work
She said, "let's go sing a song," Amen
We've got a piano there at work,
And we had a whole bunch of us there
And we started singing church songs Praise God, WHOOOOOO
You know, I feel a lot tonight
Like she did Amen, praise God!
When we got through, she said
"Hallelujah" and "Amen" and
"Let's start the shouting," Yes, Lord, hallelujah!
And you know I think if we keep praying for her
She's going to come into church
And start shouting with us Amen, amen, yes, Lord
I feel like deep down in my heart
We've got to get to singing and praying,
Everything,
Shouting for God's blessing Yes, Lord, amen
Pray for me that I'll do his will. Yes, Lord, yes

TESTIMONY 4

Truly tonight I am thankful to be able
To be in the house of the Lord.
I feel that he is here with us
To guide and direct us through our life.
Truly tonight I love the Lord
With all my heart.
I want to draw closer to him
Do what he would have me to do
And I want to go all the way with him
Is my heart's desire. Yes, Lord, amen, amen

TESTIMONY 5

I want to praise the Lord tonight. Praise His name
I know that he is real.
I know that he is a mighty friend Yes, Lord

And will stand beside me. Oh, yes
You know it makes no difference
What comes or what goes
He's going to be there beside us. Oh, yes, Lord
He'll never fail us tonight,
Just pray and be true to him and be faithful
And be ready to meet him. Thank you, Jesus
[Congregation sings "Jesus on the Main Line"; ends with clapping and shouting.]

TESTIMONY 6

You know I praise the Lord tonight
For the spirit we have here tonight
But I feel like if we just let go
We'll get more Hallelujah, WHOOOOOOO!!!
Hallelujah, yes Lord!
Hallelujah, WHOOOOOOO!!!
If we just reach out for it
And obey it Hallelujah, yes Jesus
Praise His Name, WHOOOOOOO
I praise the lord tonight.
I think we all should just stand
And lift our hands Amen, Thank you Jesus
And praise him tonight, Oh, Hallelujah,
Thank you, Jesus, WHOOOOOOOOO Oh, Hallelujah!
Thank you, Jesus
WHOOOOOOOOOOOOOO!!!!!
[Congregation begins to shout, clap, dance, stomp.]

TESTIMONY 7

Blessed Jesus. Thank you Jesus.
Tonight I love the lord.
I thank him tonight
And I praise him
Because I know he's real in my heart
This night.
As we sang that song "Jesus on the main line"

It made me think you know
When you dig around sometimes
You get down there
And you get these little streams
You know these little streams
They're just not enough
There's just not enough water there.
But when we hit that main line Yes, Lord, hallelujah
You've got plenty of water
You've got plenty
When you get Jesus on the main line
Hallelujah! Yes, Lord, hallelujah!!!
WHOOOOOOOOOOO!!!!
You've got just what you need.
You know those little trinkles
They don't do much for me Oh, thank you Jesus!
For I've been under the Holy Spout.
Hallelujah.
It does a whole lot more for me Yes, Lord
Hallelujah! Thank you, Jesus
You know I might make you stay up for a while
Because, Praise the Lord,
Hallelujah,
I know that he is real.
Whoooooooooo
Glory,
I know he is real tonight.
You know when I sing
And when I testify
Everybody looks at me
And they think I'm kind of
Peculiar.
But you know tonight
We are peculiar people.
But you know something?
I'm not ashamed of Jesus Oh, thank you, Lord, hallelujah!
Because this is the Lord
That I sing
That I testify for

That I stomp my feet for
That I clap my hands for WHOOOOOOOOOOOOO!!!!!!
It's Jesus Christ
And I love Him tonight Oh, yes, hallelujah, yes, Lord
And he is worthy
Of all praises Yes, Lord
Everything,
Everything
That we can possibly do for him
He is worthy of it
This night Yes, Lord, Hallelujah!!!
Hallelujah, Yes, Lord, Amen!
WHOOOOOOOOOOOO!!!!!!!
WHOOOOOOOOOOOOO!!!!!
[This part gets very loud, with lots of shouting. The next speaker is the pastor:]
In Jesus' name.
Let him have his way.
[Applause. Pastor speaks:]
He's wonderful. Praise God.
[Woman testifier speaks in tongues. Lines following are interpretation of tongues by the speaker of the tongues.]
[Tongues]
I say unto thee, my people, put thy trust in me and in
No other.
[Tongues]
I say put thy trust in me
[Tongues]
For I say that I will never leave thee nor will I ever
Forsake thee
[Tongues]
For I say I will go with you
Even unto the end
[Tongues]
[The general clapping, shouting, crying, dancing continue. Pastor speaks:]
Will you raise your hands and worship him.
Just raise your hands and worship God.
He's so good.

Praise God.
Thank you Lord.

TESTIMONY 8

I just want to thank him for tonight
And for Jesus. Oh, Yes
So thankful for this week's meeting
And I can feel in my soul tonight
That without Jesus
We'll never make heaven.
And my desire is just to be drawn closer
And live with him some day. Praise His Name
Oh, Jesus
Jesus, Jesus

[Responses are subdued now.]

TESTIMONY 9.

I want to thank the Lord
For everything that he's done for me. Help her, Lord
I know he's a great big God
And I just want to give him the praise. Thank you, Jesus

TESTIMONY 10.

Well, I thank the Lord tonight
That I am able to stand before him tonight.
I was just so tired and worn out tonight
I just thought I'd stay at home.
I'm glad that I'm in the house of the Lord.
Thank him for the spirit I feel here.
I'm thankful for Jesus.
Sometimes we just sit and listen to others Oh, yes
But you know what others do
Is not going to help me. Amen
You know we've got to go
Get our own soul salvation.
I want to do what the Lord

Would have me do at all times. Yes, Lord, thank you, Jesus
[Pastor speaks:]
Anyone else?
Thank the Lord for the good testimonies tonight.
I love the scripture, it says all scripture was written
By the inspiration of God.
Hallelujah.
Inspiration of God.
Hallelujah.
All scriptures written through the inspiration of God.
And it is possible for doctrine,
For truth or direction or correction or instruction in life.
Glory to God.
It shows us the way to go.
It's good for instruction in righteousness.
If we follow the good word,
We'll be all right.
Hallelujah!
We'll make it into glory.
That the man of God may be purged.
That the man of God may be purged.
May be purged.
Let's have a good song.
[Woman leads group in singing "Jesus took the burdens that I could not longer bear."]
[End transcript.]

The first testimony of this service sets the stage for the entire group of testimonies. The first woman begins her testimony with the standard "tonight I want to thank the Lord for the privilege of being in his house." She, like so many of the others, is penitent for wanting to stay home. By line 7, she has changed her normal speaking voice to a tearful, sobbing one as she asserts that she can "feel" God; she knows he's "real," both sentiments that will be repeated in subsequent testimonies. The emotional response of her audience to these key phrases of her testimony confirm her own belief and theirs: their shared, communal emotion becomes the proof of God's existence and the sign that he is present in the room. Although her testimony relies heavily on formulaic phrases, her delivery is powerfully effective and elicits shouts, moans, groans, "Hallelujahs," and "Amens" from the others.

Testimony 2 repeats the confessions of Testimony 1. This woman, also, could be elsewhere, but church is really where she ought to be and, above all, where she wants to be, mainly because she believes the "blessing" she might get—that is, the communal reaffirmation of God's existence and her participation in it, which will insure his help to her—will get her "through next week." For her, it seems the litany of what she needs will become a reality if she but states it:

I know he's never going to try me
Or try to pull me down.
He's going to work with me
And he's going to put his arms close around me.
But I know tonight
That my blessings tonight
Are going to pull me through next week.
I'm going to be safe.

The trials of "next week" are graphically contrasted with the glorious heaven that she and her cobelievers can't even imagine because their "minds are so small." Her "truly tonight, I love the Lord and I want to go all the way with him" is formulaic, but is at the same time her personal claim that she recognizes God's power and knows what she must do to gain approval and gain heaven. Although this woman does not become tearful during her delivery or rely on a chanted style, there is much in this testimony that the others in the congregation can relate to and the energetic responses attest to the important communal core that has been touched.

By Testimony 3 it is obvious that this testimony service will go beyond the simple recitation of formulaic obligations to testify. Each testimony given thus far has exhibited personal interjection and creativity. Testimony 3 begins with the standard formula "Truly tonight I want to thank God for all that he's done for me" and immediately rejects further formula for the narration of a personal experience story. Her story is meant not only to show that she has been witnessing to a co-worker, but to make the point that the folks in the church ought to be doing more shouting if they expect to get God's blessing:

I feel like deep down in my heart
We've got to get to singing and praying,
Everything,
Shouting for God's blessing.

At this point the group heeds her message and begins to shout loudly. A portion of her testimony is lost in the noise of the congregation. As the shouting dies down, her closing lines are clear and predictable: "Pray for me that I'll do his will."

Testimonies 4 and 5 are quietly rendered, entirely formulaic testimonies. During these testimonies there is no "shouting" in the church, but the mood has most definitely been influenced by the more dramatic testimonies. The lull holds the promise of more to come, the low groans, moans and crying "thank you Jesus" anticipate further group stimulation.

Following Testimony 5, the group sings "Jesus on the Main Line," a popular song at this church, a rousing song with the possibility of endless verses:

If you want the Holy Ghost,
Tell him what you want.
If you want the Holy Ghost,

Tell him what you want.
If you want the Holy Ghost,
Tell him what you want.
Jesus on the main line, now.
Chorus: Call him up, Call him up,
Tell him what you want.
Call him up, Call him up,
Tell him what you want.
Call him up, call him up,
Tell him what you want.
Jesus on the main line, now.
Other stanzas: If you need a healing, now, etc.

When the congregation at Johnson's Creek sings this song, they repeat it again and again as they march around the church, in and out of the pews; women get tambourines and members dance at their places in the pews or go to the front to dance. Any member can initiate a new verse and the others will take her cue and sing with her. It is the type of song the members rely on to build excitement. The words are simple to learn and everyone can participate. Following the last verse sung, the group applauds and shouts.

The next testifier sees the potential for increasing the stimulation already evident in the group and calls for the members to "let go" even more. She demonstrates for them as she shouts, claps, dances around the church. This woman is a creative, spontaneous testifier who fully realizes her own potential for power within the testimony frame. She knows that the group has reached a high level of excitement and she proceeds to take them to the peak of ecstatic involvement. She is aware of the demands on her performance in terms of structure, content, and delivery style.

The testimony services, such as the one given above, serve to reaffirm to the entire group, male and female, that God is real. The recognized powers of the women are allowed to serve this endeavor. But the tongue-speaking episode of the service is followed by the restoration of authority into the hands of the pastor. He signals that the testimony service must come to a close, that it is time to alter the tenor of the service. In a calm, normal speaking voice he regains control of the service, thanking the Lord for the "good testimonies" and calling for a "good song."

Notes

PREFACE

1. Related by a sixty-five-year-old woman, interviewed July 14, 1980, in her home at Bloomington, Indiana, by folklorist Elizabeth Peterson and me. Quotations in this book are all from Pentecostal women and men in southern Indiana from 1977 through 1981; some of the interviews were videotaped while Peterson and I were working on the documentary *Joy Unspeakable*. Because of the sensitive nature of this material on religious belief, no actual names of living persons will be used; the names of the churches mentioned in this book have also been changed to protect their privacy. The actual names of counties and towns in Indiana, however, have been retained. All audio tapes and transcriptions of the videotapes are on file in my private archives at the University of Missouri. Henceforth in this work, information about informants and the circumstances of interviews will be provided only when needed to enhance understanding.

2. Examinations of the birth and development of Pentecostalism include: Walter Hollenweger, *The Pentecostals* (Minneapolis; Augsburg Publishing House, 1972); Robert Mapes Anderson, *Vision of the Disinherited* (New York: Oxford University Press, 1979); Nils Block-Hoell, *The Pentecostal Movement* (Oslo: Scandinavian University Books, 1964); Vinson Synan, *The Holiness-Pentecostal Movement in the United States* (Grand Rapids: Wm. B. Eerdmans Publishing Co., 1971); John Nicol, *Pentecostalism* (New York: Harper & Row, 1966); and David Harrell, Jr., *All Things Are Possible* (Bloomington: Indiana University Press, 1975).

3. See William Samarin, *Tongues of Men and Angels: The Religious Language of Pentecostalism* (New York: Macmillan Co., 1972); George B. Cutten, *Speaking With Tongues* (New Haven: Yale University Press, 1927); Morton Kelsey, *Tongue Speaking* (New York: Doubleday & Co,,

1964); and John L. Sherrill, *They Speak with Other Tongues* (New York: McGraw Hill Book Co., 1964).

4. For example, the large and influential United Pentecostal Church is a Oneness Pentecostal church. Many small churches are loosely associated with that umbrella organization, but even more small congregations are not affiliated with any recognized organization. My own recent fieldwork in central and southern Missouri supports the contention that conservative, fundamentalist religion and Pentecostalism in particular are strong and growing.

5. See Dell Hymes, "Ethnography of Speaking," in *Anthropology and Human Behavior*, ed. T. Gladwin and William Sturtevant (Washington: Anthropological Society, 1962); "Ethnography of Communication," *American Anthropologist* 66:1-34; "Sociolinguistics and the Ethnography of Speaking," in *Social Anthropology and Language*, ed. Edwin Ardener (London: Tavistock, 1971).

6. For discussions of verbal art in performance, see Richard Bauman, *Verbal Art as Performance* (Rowley: Newbury House, 1977); and Elaine J. Lawless, "Oral 'Character' and Literary 'Art': A Call for a New Reciprocity between Oral Literature and Folklore," *Western Folklore* 44 (April 1985):77-97.

7. Religious scholars concerned with religion and gender have always acknowledged the predominance of women in religious contexts. See, for example, Janet Wilson James, ed., *Women in American Religion* (Philadelphia: University of Pennsylvania Press, 1980).

8. At this time, only a few folklorists had turned their scholarly attentions to American fundamentalist religion. See Jeff Titon, "Some Recent Pentecostal Revivals: A Report in Words and Photographs," *Georgia Review* 32 (Fall, 1978):579-605; Titon and Ken George, "Testimonies: Transcribed Testimonies of Rachel Franklin, Edith Cubbage, Rev. John Sherfey," *Alcheringa* 4 (1978):69-83; Beverly Boggs, "Some Aspects of Worship in a Holiness Church," *New York Folklore Quarterly* 3 (Summer-Winter, 1977):29-45; William Clements, *The American Folk Church*, Ph.D. Diss., Indiana University, 1974; and Bruce Rosenberg, *The Art of the American Folk Preacher* (New York: Oxford University Press, 1970).

9. The production of the television video-documentary, *Joy Unspeakable*, was supported by the Indiana Committee on the Humanities, the Folklore Institute of Indiana University, and Indiana University Radio and Television. The documentary, which won a red ribbon award from the American Film Festival in 1981 and has aired on PBS, was directed by Indiana University producer John Winninger, and is available from the Indiana University Film Distribution Center.

10. James Agee, *Let Us Now Praise Famous Men* (Boston: Houghton Mifflin, 1939), p. 7.

INTRODUCTION

1. Attention to Pentecostalism has been particularly biased toward the more sensational aspects of Appalachian congregations that handle snakes and drink strychnine as a regular part of their religious services. See Ellen Steckert, "The Snake-Handling Sect of Harlan County, Kentucky," *Southern Folklore Quarterly* 27 (1963):316-22; Western LaBarre, *They Shall Take Up Serpents* (Minneapolis: University of Minnesota Press, 1962); Steven Kane, "Ritual Possession in a Southern Appalachian Religious Sect," *Journal of American Folklore* 87 (October-December, 1974):293-303; Berthold Schwartz, "Ordeal by Serpents, Fire and Strychnine," *Psychiatric Quarterly* 34 (1960):405-29; and Nathan L. Gerrard, "The Serpent-Handling Religions of West Virginia," *TransActions* 5 (1968):22-38.

For definitions of a "folk church" or "folk religion" see Don Yoder, "Toward a Definition of Folk Religion," *Western Folklore* 33 (1974):2-16; Yoder, "Official Religion vs. Folk Religion," *Pennsylvania Folklife* 15 (1966): 36-52; William Clements, "The American Folk Church," (Ph.D. Diss., Indiana University, 1974); and Clements, "The American Folk Church in Northeastern Arkansas," *Journal of the Folklore Institute* 15:161-80.

2. For studies of preaching see Bruce Rosenberg, *The Art of the American Folk Preacher* (New York: Oxford University Press, 1970); Rosenberg, "Oral Sermons and Oral Narrative," in *Folklore, Performance and Communication*, ed. Dan Ben-Amos and Kenneth Goldstein (The Hague: Mouton, 1975), pp. 76-106; Rosenberg, "The Oral Quality of Rev. Shegog's Sermon in William Faulkner's *The Sound and the Fury*," *Literature in Wissenschaft und Unterricht* 2(1969):73-88; Rosenberg, "The Formulaic Quality of Spontaneous Sermons," *Journal of American Folklore* 83(1970):3-20; Jeff Titon and Ken George, "Dressed in the Armor of God," *Alcheringa/Ethnopoetics* 3(1977):10-19; Peter Gold, "Easter Sunrise Sermon," Alcheringa/Ethnopoetics 4(1972):1-14. For examinations of women's preaching styles see Elaine J. Lawless, "Oral 'Character' and 'Literary' Art"; Lawless, "Traditional Women Preachers in Mid-Missouri," *Missouri Folklore Society Journal* 6 (1984):47-60; Lawless, "Tradition and Poetics: The Sermons of Women Preachers," in *A Memorial for Milman Parry*, ed. John M. Foley (Columbus, Ohio: Slavica Press, 1987); and *Handmaidens of the Lord: Pentecostal Women*

Preachers and Traditional Religion (Philadelphia: University of Pennsylvania Press, 1988), forthcoming; and Gerald Davis, *I Got the Word in Me and I Can Sing It, You Know* (Philadelphia: University of Pennsylvania Press, 1986). For studies on testimony, see Jeff Titon and Ken George, "Testimonies: Transcribed testimonies of Rachel Franklin, Edith Cubbage, Rev. John Sherfey," *Alcheringa* 4 (1978):69-83; Elaine J. Lawless, " 'I Know if I Don't Bear my Testimony I'll Lose It': Mormon Women's Testimonies," *Kentucky Folklore Quarterly* 30 (1984):113-27; J. Stephen Kroll-Smith, "The Testimony as Performance: The Relationship of an Expressive Event to the Belief System of a Holiness Sect," *Journal for the Scientific Study of Religion* 16 (1977):165-69. For the best survey of folksong scholarship, including religious song and music, see D.K. Wilgus, *Anglo-American Folksong Scholarship Since 1898* (New Brunswick, N.J.: Rutgers University Press, 1959). See also George P. Jackson, *White Spirituals in the Southern Uplands* (Chapel Hill: University of North Carolina Press, 1933). On healing see William Clements, "Faith-healing Narratives from Northeast Arkansas," *Indiana Folklore* 9 (1976):15-39; and "Ritual Expectation in Pentecostal Healing Experience," *Western Folklore* 40 (1981):139-48.

3. Typical of the anthropological works that folklorists rely on in defining and discussing folk religion are: Charles Leslie, *Anthropology of Folk Religion* (New York: Random House, 1960); David K. Jordan, *Gods, Ghosts, and Ancestors: Folk Religion in a Taiwanese Village* (Berkeley: University of California Press, 1972); Michael Banton, *Anthropological Approaches to the Study of Religion* (New York: Tavistock Pub., 1966); and William A. Lessa and Evon Z. Vogt, *Reader in Comparative Religion: An Anthropological Approach* (New York: Harper and Row, 1979). None of these references, however, treat modern American fundamentalist religions.

4. John Messenger, "Folk Religion," in *Folkore and Folklife*, ed. Richard Dorson (Chicago: University of Chicago Press, 1972), pp. 222, 220.

5. Yoder, "Toward a Definition," pp. 5, 7.

6. Quoted by Yoder, "Toward a Definition," pp. 6, 8.

7. Dov Noy, "Is there a Jewish Folk Religion?" in *Studies in Jewish Folklore*, ed. Frank Talmage (Cambridge, Mass.: Association for Jewish Studies, 1980), pp. 273-87.

8. Clements, "The American Folk Church," p. 163.

9. See Barre Toelken, *The Dynamics of Folklore* (Boston: Houghton Mifflin Co., 1979), p. 35.

10. Bruce Rosenberg, *The Art of the American Folk Preacher* (New York: Oxford University Press, 1970); Gerald Davis, *I Got the Word*

in Me And I Can Sing It, You Know (Philadelphia: University of Pennsylvania Press, 1985).

11. Jeff Titon, "Powerhouse for God: Sacred Speech, Chant, and Song in an Appalachian Baptist Church," booklet and record, American Folklore Recordings, Daniel W. Patterson, Ed. (Chapel Hill: University of North Carolina Press, 1982).

12. See Diane E. Goldstein "The Language of Religious Experience and Its Implications for Fieldwork," *Western Folklore* 42 (1983):105-13.

13. Albert B. Lord, *The Singer of Tales* (New York: Atheneum, 1976; first pub. Harvard Universiy Press, 1960).

1. THE FIELD SITUATION

1. See Dickson Bruce, *And They All Sang Hallelujah, Plain-Folk Camp-Meeting Religion, 1800-1845* (Knoxville: University of Tennessee Press, 1974), for an excellent survey of the early camp meeting tradition. See also Bernard A. Weisberger, *They Gathered at the River* (Chicago: Quadrangle Books, 1958); Melvin Dieter, *The Holiness Revival of the Nineteenth Century* (New Jersey: Scarecrow Press, 1980); Charles Johnson, *The Frontier Camp Meeting* (Dallas: Southern Methodist University Press, 1955); Catherine Cleveland, *The Great Revival in the West, 1797-1805* (Chicago: University of Chicago Press, 1916); William Warren Sweet, *Religion on the American Frontier* (New York: Henry Holt and Co., 1931); and Samuel S. Hill, Jr., ed., *Religion and the Solid South* (Nashville: Abingdon Press, 1972) and *Southern Churches in Crisis* (New York: Holt, Rinehart and Winston, 1966).

2. For clarification see Nathan L. Gerrard, "The Holiness Movement in Southern Appalachia," in Michael P. Hamilton, ed., *The Charismatic Movement* (Grand Rapids: Eerdmans, 1975).

3. See the chart developed by Nils Block-Hoell, *The Pentecostal Movement* (Oslo, Norway: Universitetsforlaget, 1964), pp. 58-69. Although dated and incomplete, the chart does help identify common names of Pentecostal churches.

4. Vinson Synan, *The Holiness-Pentecostal Movement in the United States* (Grand Rapids: Eerdmans, 1971), p. 14.

5. John Nichol, *Pentecostalism* (New York: Harper and Row, 1966), p. 6.

6. See W.J. Hollenweger, *The Pentecostals* (Minneapolis: Augsberg, 1972), p. 406, for a discussion of this phenomenon.

7. Synan, *Holiness-Pentecostal Movement*, p. 66.

8. For several variant accounts of the story of how Parham's followers came up with this answer on their own while Parham was out of town, see Synan, *Holiness-Pentecostal Movement*, p. 101; Nichol, *Pentecostalism*, p. 27; and Block-Hoell, *Pentecostal Movement*, p. 19.

9. Nichol, *Pentecostalism*, p. 8.

10. Nichol, *Pentecostalism*, p. 92.

11. Hollenweger cites this as the birthplace of the worldwide Pentecostal movement in *The Pentecostals*, p. 22.

12. Block-Hoell, *Pentecostal Movement*, p. 52.

13. Synan, *Holiness-Pentecostal Movement*, p. 154.

2. MAINTAINING BOUNDARIES

1. See Luther P. Gerlach and Virginia H. Hine, "Five Factors Crucial to the Growth and Spread of a Modern Religious Movement," *Journal for the Scientific Study of Religion* 7 (1968):36-7; and R. A. Schermerhorn, "Ethnicity in the Perspective of the Sociology of Knowledge," *Ethnicity* 1 (1974):1.

2. For discussion of what a folk group is and how group identity is established and maintained, see Alan Dundes, "What is Folklore?" and William Jansen, "The Esoteric-Exoteric Factor in Folklore," in *The Study of Folklore*, ed. Alan Dundes (Englewood Cliffs, N.J.: Prentice-Hall, 1965).

3. Max Weber, *The Sociology of Religion* (Boston: Beacon Press, 1922), p. 108.

4. Much of my discussion of religious boundaries has been based on Fredrik Barth's notions of ethnic boundaries in *Ethnic Groups and Boundaries* (Boston: Little, Brown and Co., 1969).

5. Gerlach and Hine, "Five Factors," p. 30.

3. DISCOURSE RULES

1. I am, of course, using terms such as "performance" in the way Richard Bauman has suggested in his *Verbal Art as Performance* (Rowley, Mass.: Newbury House, 1977). Bauman also discusses the role in performance of a critical audience.

2. John Holmes McDowell, "The Corrido of Greater Mexico," in *"And Other Neighborly Names": Social Process and Cultural Image in Texas Folklore*, ed. Richard Bauman and Roger D. Abrahams (Austin: University of Texas Press, 1981) p. 71.

3. For explications of the uses of these terms see Dell Hymes, "Models of the Interaction of Language and Social Setting," in the *Journal of Social Issues* 23 (1967):8-28; Robert T. Bell, *Sociolinguistics* (London: B.T. Batsford LTD, 1976), pp. 28-60; Erving Goffman, *Frame Analysis* (New York: Harper and Row, 1974); and John Austin, *How To Do Things with Words* (Cambridge, Mass.: Harvard University Press, 1962).

4. See Susan Ervin-Tripp, "On Sociolinguistic Rules: Alternation and Co-Occurrence," in *Directions in Sociolinguistics*, eds. J. J. Gumperz and Dell Hymes (New York: Holt, Rinehart and Winston, 1972), pp. 213-50.

5. The "Schema of Speech Acts" developed for the religious service at Johnson's Creek Church, reflected in Tables 1-4, but especially in Table 1, is based on Hymes's mnemonic device SPEAKING as outlined in his numerous explications toward "an ethnography of communication." See Dell Hymes, "Ethnography of Speaking," in *Anthropology and Human Behavior*, ed. T. Gladwin and W. Sturtevant (Washington D.C.: Anthropological Society, 1962); Hymes, "The Anthropology of Communication," in *Human Communication Theory*, ed. Frank E.X. Dance (New York: Holt, Rinehart and Winston, 1967); and Hymes, "The Ethnography of Speaking," in *Language, Culture and Society*, ed. Ben Blount (Cambridge, Winthrop 1974).

6. For an explanation of the folklorist's use of the terms "emic" and "etic," see Alan Dundes, "From Etic to Emic Units inthe Structural Study of Folktales," in *Analytic Essays in Folklore*, ed. Alan Dundes (The Hague: Mouton, 1975), pp. 61-73. See also Dell Hymes, *Foundations in Sociolinguistics* (Philadelphia: University of Pennsylvania Press, 1975), p. 11.

7. See I.T. Ramsey, *Religious Language* (London: SCM Press, 1957).

8. William T. Blackstone, "The Status of God-Talk," in *Religious Language and Knowledge*, ed. Robert H. Ayers and William T. Blackstone (Athens: University of Georgia Press, 1972), p. 4.

9. Hymes, "Ethnography of Speaking," pp. 28-39.

10. For an explanation of the "ethnography of speaking" school's use of Bateson's term "frame," see Richard Bauman and J. Sherzer, "The Ethnography of Speaking," in *Annual Review of Anthropology*, ed. Bernard Seigal (1976), pp. 105-06.

11. Bauman, *Verbal Art as Performance*, p. 11.

12. Bauman and Sherzer, "Explorations in the Ethnography of Speaking," p. 6.

4. POWER OF THE WORD

1. I have recently completed a study of Pentecostal women preachers, *Handmaidens of the Lord: Pentecostal Women Preachers and Traditional Religion*, which will be published by the Publications of the American Folklore Society and the University of Pennsylvania Press in 1988.

2. Barre Toelken, *The Dynamics of Folklore* (Boston: Houghton Mifflin, 1979), p. 35.

3. I.M. Lewis, *Ecstatic Religion* (Middlesex, Eng.: Penguin, 1971).

4. Robin Lakoff, *Language and Woman's Place* (New York: Harper & Row, 1975), p. 1.

5. Lakoff, *Language*, p. 7.

6. John Holmes McDowell, "The Corrido of Greater Mexico," in "*And Other Neighborly Names*", ed. Richard Bauman and Roger D. Abrahams (Austin: University of Texas Press, 1981), p. 50.

7. See Dennis Tedlock, "On the Translation of Style in Oral Narrative," in *Toward New Perspectives in Folklore*, ed. Americo Paredes and Richard Bauman (Austin: University of Texas Press, 1972), pp. 114-33.

8. Cf. Dell Hymes, *"In Vain I Tried to Tell You": Essays in Native American Ethnopoetics* (Philadelphia: University of Pennsylvania Press, 1981).

9. Roman Jakobson, "Closing Statement: Linguistics and Poetics," in *Style in Language*, ed. Thomas A. Sebeok (Cambridge: MIT Press, 1960), p. 354.

10. Jakobson, "Closing Statement," p. 355.

11. Bruce Rosenberg, *The Art of the American Folk Preacher* (Oxford: Oxford University Press, 1970), p. 43.

12. Rosenberg, *Art* pp. 30-33.

13. For a discussion of the semiotic function of religious behaviors, see Elaine J. Lawless, " 'What Did She Say?' An Application of Peirce's General Theory of Signs to Glossolalia in the Pentecostal Religion," *Folklore Forum* 3:23-39.

Bibliography

Abrahams, Roger. "Folklore and Literature as Performance." *Journal of the Folklore Institute* 4 (1967):75-95.

———. "Introductory Remarks to a Rhetorical Theory of Folklore." *Journal of American Folklore* 81 (1968):143-58.

———. "Personal Power and Social Restraint in the Definition of Folklore." *Journal of American Folklore* 84 (1971):16-30.

———. "Folklore and Literature as Performance." *Journal of the Folklore Institute* 8 (1971):75-94.

———. "Folklore in the Definition of Ethnicity: An American and Jewish Perspective." In *Studies in Jewish Folklore*, ed. Frank Talmage. Cambridge: Association for Jewish Studies, 1980.

Alland, Alexander. "Possession in a Revivalistic Negro Church." *Journal for the Scientific Study of Religion* 1 (1962):204-13.

Allardt, E. "Approaches in the Socialization of Religion." *Temenos* 6 (1970):10-12.

Allison, J. "Religious Conversion: Regression and Progression in an Adolescent Experience." *Journal for the Scientific Study of Religion* 8 (1969):23-38.

Anderson, Robert Mapes. *Vision of the Disinherited*. New York: Oxford University Press, 1979.

Ardener, Edwin. "Belief and the Problem of Women." In *The Interpretation of Ritual*, ed. J. S. LaFontaine, pp. 135-159. London: Tavistock, 1972.

Ardener, Shirley. *Perceiving Women*. London: J.M. Dent, 1975.

Arnold, Matthew. "Religious Language is Moral-emotive." In *The Problem of Religious Language*, ed. M. J. Charlesworth. Englewood Cliffs: Prentice-Hall, 1974.

Austin, John. *How To Do Things with Words*. Cambridge: Harvard University Press, 1962.

Ayers, Robert H. and William T. Blackstone. *Religious Language and Knowledge*. Athens: University of Georgia Press, 1972.

Baal, J. Van. *Symbols for Communication: An Introduction to the Anthropological Study of Religion*. Assen, The Netherlands: Van Gorcum, 1971.

Babcock, Barbara, ed. *The Reversible World*. New York: Cornell University Press, 1978.

Banton, Michael. *Anthropological Approaches to the Study of Religion*. New York: Tavistock, 1966.

Barnes, Douglas F. "Charisma and Religious Leadership." *Journal for the Scientific Study of Religion* 17 (1978):1-19.

Barth, Fredrik. *Ethnic Groups and Boundaries*. Boston: Little, Brown, 1969.

Basso, Keith H. and Henry A. Selby, eds. *Meaning in Anthropology*. Albuquerque: University of New Mexico Press, 1976.

Bascom, William. "Verbal Art." *Journal of American Folklore* 68 (1955):245-62.

Batson, C. Daniel. "Religion as Prosocial: Agent or Double Agent?" *Journal for the Scientific Study of Religion* 16 (1977):29-45.

Bauman, Richard. "Aspects of Quaker Rhetoric." *Quarterly Journal of Speech* 56 (1971):67-74.

———. "Differential Identity and the Social Base of Folklore." In *New Perspectives in Folklore*, ed. Americo Paredes and Richard Bauman, pp. 31-42. Austin: University of Texas Press, 1972.

——— and Joel Sherzer. *Explorations in the Ethnography of Speaking*. New York: Cambridge University Press, 1974.

———. *Verbal Art as Performance*. Rowley: Newbury House, 1977.

———. "The Field Study of Folklore in Context." In *The Handbook of American Folklore*, ed. Richard M. Dorson, pp. 362-69. Bloomington: Indiana University Press, 1983.

Bell, Roger T. *Sociolinguistics*. London: B.T. Batsford, 1976.

Beit-Hallahmi, Benjamin, ed. *Research in Religious Behavior*. Boston: Brooks/Cole, 1973.

Ben-Amos, Dan. "Toward a Definition of Folklore in Context." In *Toward New Perspectives in Folklore*. Austin: University of Texas Press, 1972.

——— and Kenneth Goldstein. *Folklore, Performance and Communication*. The Hague: Mouton, 1974.

Blackstone, William T. "The Status of God-Talk." In *Religious Language and Knowledge*, ed. Robert H. Ayers and William T. Blackstone. Athens: University of Georgia Press, 1972.

Block-Hoell, Nils. *The Pentecostal Movement*. Oslo, Norway: Universitetsforlaget, 1964.

Blount, Ben G. *Language, Culture and Society*. Cambridge, Mass: Winthrop, 1974.

Boatright, Mody C. "Comic Exempla of the Pioneer Pulpit." In *Coyote Wisdom*, ed. J. Frank Dobie, M. Boatright, and Harry H. Ransom. Austin: Texas Folklore Society 14 (1963):55-68.

Boggs, Beverly. "Some Aspects of Worship in a Holiness Church." *New York Folklore Quarterly* 3 (1947):29-45.

Boisen, Anton T. *Religion in Crises and Custom*. New York: Harper, 1955.

———. "Economic Distress and Religious Experience: A Study of the Holy Rollers." *Psychiatry* 2 (1939):185-94.

———. "Religion and Hard Times: A Study of the Holy Rollers." *Social Action* 39 (1972):8-35.

Bourguignon, Erika. *Religion, Altered States of Consciousness and Social Change*. Columbus: Ohio State University Press, 1973.

———. "Cross-cultural Perspectives on the Religious Uses of Altered States of Consciousness." In *Religious Movements in Contemporary America*, ed. Irving L. Zaretsky, pp. 228-44. Princeton: Princeton University Press, 1974.

———. *A World of Women: Anthropological Studies of Women in the Societies of the World*. New York: Praeger, 1980.

Brouwer, D. and M. Gerritsen. "Speech Differences between Women and Men: On the Right Track?" *Language in Society* 8 (1979):33-51.

Bruce, Dickson. *And They All Sang Hallelujah:Plain-Folk Camp-Meeting Religion, 1800-1845*. Knoxville: University of Tennessee Press, 1974.

Bruner, Frederick D. *A Theology of the Holy Spirit*. Grand Rapids: Eerdmans, 1970.

Brunvand, Jan. "Jokes About Misunderstood Religious Texts." *Western Folklore* 24 (1965):199-200.

Burr, Nelson. *A Critical Bibliography of Religion in America*. Princeton: Princeton University Press, 1961.

Byrne, Donald. *No Foot of Land*. New Jersey: Scarecrow Press, 1975.

Caillois, Roger. "Play and the Sacred." In *Man and the Sacred*, ed. Roger Caillois. Glencoe, Ill: Free Press, 1959.

Caplow, Theodore, etal. *All Faithful People: Change and Continuity in Middletown's Religion*. Minneapolis: University of Minnesota Press, 1983.

Capps, Donald. "Publishing Trends in the Psychology of Religion to 1974." *Journal for the Scientific Study of Religion* 15 (1976):15-28.

Carr, Leslie G. and William Hanser. "Anomie and Religiosity: An Empirical Re-Examination." *Journal for the Scientific Study of Religion* 15 (1976):26-42.

Catton, William R. "What Kinds of People Does a Religious Cult Attract?" *American Sociological Review* 22 (1957):561-66.

Charlesworth, M.J., ed. *The Problem of Religious Language*. Englewood Cliffs: Prentice-Hall, 1974.

Christ, Carol and Judith Plaskow, eds. *Womanspirit Rising*. San Francisco: Harper & Row, 1979.

Christie-Murray, David. *Voices from the Gods*. London: Routledge and Kegan Paul, 1978.

Cicourel, Aaron W. "Basic and Normative Rules in the Negotiation of Status and Role." In *Studies in Social Interaction*, ed. David Sudnow. Englewood Cliffs: Prentice-Hall, 1972.

Clanton, Arthur L. *United We Stand*. Hazelwood, Mo.: The Pentecostal Publishing House, 1970.

Clark, Elmer T. *The Small Sects in America*. Nashville: Abingdon, 1959.

Clements, William. "The Rhetoric of the Radio Ministry." *Journal of American Folklore* 87 (1974):318-27.

———. "The American Folk Church." Ph.D. dissertation, Indiana University, 1974.

———. "Conversion and Communitas." *Western Folklore* 35 (1976):35-45.

———. "Faith Healing Narratives from Northeast Arkansas." *Indiana Folklore* 9 (1976):15-39.

———. "the American Folk Church in Northeastern Arkansas" *Journal of the Folklore Institute* 15 (1978):161-80.

——— "Ritual Expectations in Pentecostal Healing Experience." *Western Folklore* 40 (1981):139-48.

———. "The Folk Church: Institution, Event, Performance." In *The Handbook of American Folklore*, ed. Richard M. Dorson, Bloomington: Indiana University Press, 1983.

———. "Public Testimony as Oral Performance: A Study in the Ethnography of Religious Speaking." *Linguistica Biblica* 47 (1980):21-32.

Cleveland, Catherine. *The Great Revival in the West, 1797-1805*. Chicago: University of California Press, 1916.

Cohn, Norman. *The Pursuit of the Millennium*. New York: Oxford Univ. Press, 1970.

Collins, J.B. *Tennessee Snake Handlers*. Chattanooga: Middle Tennessee State University Press, 1947.

Cone, James H. "Sanctification, Liberation, and Black Worship." *Theology Today* 35 (1979):139-50.

Cox, Harvey. *The Feast of Fools*. New York: Harper & Row, 1969.
———. *The Seduction of the Spirit: The Use and Misuse of People's Religion*. New York: Simon and Schuster, 1973.
Crick, Malcolm. *Explorations in Language and Meaning*. London: Malaby Press, 1976.
Crites, Stephen. "The Narrative Quality of Experience." *Journal of the American Academy of Religion* 39 (1971):291-311.
Crystal, David. *Linguistics, Language and Religion*. New York: Hawthorn, 1965.
Cutten, George B. *Speaking With Tongues*. New Haven: Yale University Press, 1927.
Daly, Mary. *Beyond God the Father*. Boston: Beacon Press, 1973.
Damboriena, Prudencio. *Tongues as of Fire: Pentecostalism in Contemporary Christianity*. Cleveland: Corpus Books, 1969.
Davis, Gerald R. *I Got the Word in Me and I Can Sing It, You Know*. Philadelphia: University of Pennsylvania Press, 1985.
Dieter, Melvin. *The Holiness Revival of the Nineteenth Century*. New Jersey: Scarecrow Press, 1980.
Doely, Sarah Bentley, ed. *Women's Liberation and the Church*. New York: Association Press, 1970.
Donovan, Peter. *Religious Language*. London: Sheldon, 1976.
Douglas, Ann. *The Feminization of American Culture*. New York: Avon, 1977.
Douglas, Mary. *Purity and Danger*. London: Routledge & Kegan Paul, 1966.
———. *Implicit Meanings*. London: Routledge & Kegan Paul, 1975.
Drake, St. Clair and Horace R. Clayton. *Black Metropolis*. New York: Harper and Row, 1962.
Dundes, Alan. "Trends in Content Analysis: A Review Article." *Midwest Folklore* 12 (1962):31-38.
———. "From Etic to Emic Units in the Structure of Folktales." In *Analytic Essays in Folklore*, ed. Alan Dundes, pp. 61-73. The Hague: Mouton, 1975.
———. "Metafolklore and Oral Literary Criticism." In *Analytic Essays in Folklore*, ed. Alan Dundes, pp. 50-61. The Hague: Mouton, 1975.
———. "Text, Texture and Context." In *Interpreting Folklore*, ed. Alan Dundes, pp. 20-33. Bloomington: Indiana University Press, 1980.
Dunn, Mary M. "Saints and Sisters: Congregational and Quaker Women in the Early Colonial Period." In *Women in American Religion*, ed. Janet James. Philadelphia: University of Pennsylvania Press, 1980.
Durasoff, Steve. *Bright Wind of the Spirit*. Englewood Cliffs, N.J.: Prentice-Hall, 1972.

Dworkin, Andrea. *Woman Hating*. New York: E. P. Dutton, 1974.
Elverdam, Beth. "Where Men and Women Have Separate Worlds—How Ritual is Used as a Mechanism of Socialization." *Temenos* 13 (1977):56-66.
Ervin-Tripp, Susan. "On Sociolinguistic Rules: Alternations and Co-Occurrance." In *Directions in Sociolinguistics*, ed. J.J. Gumperz and Dell Hymes, pp. 213-50. New York: Holt, Rinehart and Winston, 1972.
———. "Sociolinguistics." In *Language, Culture and Society*, ed. Ben G. Blount, pp. 268-334. Cambridge, Mass: Winthrop, 1974.
Falk, Nancy A. and Rita M. Gross. *Unspoken Worlds: Women's Religious Lives in Non-Western Cultures*. San Franciso: Harper & Row, 1980.
Farb, Peter. *Word Play*. New York: Alfred Knopf, 1974.
Fauset, Arthur Huff. *Black Gods of the Metropolis*. Philadelphia: University of Pennsylvania Press, 1944.
Fernandez, James. "Revitalized Words from 'The Parrot's Egg' and 'The Bull that Crashes in the Kraal': African Cult Sermons." In *Essays on the Verbal and Visual Arts*, ed. June Helm, pp. 45-63. Seattle: University of Washington Press, 1967.
———. "The Mission of Metaphor in Expressive Culture." *Current Anthropology* 15 (1974):119-33.
Ferris, William. "The Rose Hill Service." *Mississippi Folklore Register* 6 (1972):37-56.
Festinger, Leon. *When Prophecy Fails*. New York: Harper Torchbooks, 1964.
Fischer, Clare Benedicks, Betsy Brenneman, and Anne McGrew Bennett, eds. *Women in a Strange Land*. Philadelphia: Fortress Press, 1975.
Fishman, Joshua. *Advances in the Sociology of Language*. The Hague: Mouton, 1971.
———. "Domains and the Relationships Between Micro-and Macro-sociolinguistics." In *Directions in Sociolinguistics*, ed. J.J. Gumperz and Dell Hymes. New York: Holt, Rinehart and Winston, 1972.
Ford, T. "Status, Residence and Fundamentalist Religious Beliefs in the Southern Appalachians." *Social Forces* 39 (1960):41-9.
Frodsham, Stanley H. "*With Signs Following*". Springfield, Mo: Gospel Publishing House, 1926.
Gage, Miltalda Joslyn. *Woman, Church and State*. New York: Arno Press, 1972.
Gee, Donald. *The Pentecostal Movement*. London: Elim Publishing House, 1949.
Geertz, Clifford. "Religion as a Cultural System." In *The Interpretation*

of Cultures, ed. Clifford Geertz, pp. 87-126. New York: Basic Books, 1973.

George, Kenneth. " 'I've Still Got It': The Conversion Narrative of John C. Sherley." M.A. thesis, Univ. of North Carolina, 1978.

Gerlach, Luther P. and Virginia H. Hine. "Five Factors Crucial to the Growth and Spread of a Modern Religious Movement." *Journal for the Scientific Study of Religion* 7 (1968):36-47.

———. *People, Power, Change: Movements of Social Transformation*. New York: Bobbs-Merrill, 1970.

Gerrard, Nathan. "The Serpent-Handling Religions of West Virginia." *TransActions* 5 (1968):22-38.

———. "The Holiness Movement in Southern Appalachia." In *The Charismatic Movement*, ed. Michael P. Hamilton. Grand Rapids: Eerdmans, 1975.

Gibbons, Don and James deJarnette. "Hypnotic Susceptivity and Religious Experience." *Journal for the Scientific Study of Religion* 11 (1972):152-57.

Giglioli, Pier Paolo. *Language and Social Context*. New York: Penguin, 1972.

Gilmore, Susan K. "Personality Differences Between High and Low Dogmatism Groups of Pentecostal Believers." *Journal for the Scientific Study of Religion* 8 (1969):161-66.

Goffman, Erving. *Encounters*. Indianapolis: Bobbs-Merrill, 1961.

———. *Behavior in Public Places*. New York: Free Press, 1963.

———. *Interactional Ritual*. New York: Doubleday and Co., 1967.

———. "The Neglected Situation." In *Language and Social Context*, ed. Pier Paolo Giglioti, pp. 61-66. New York: Penguin, 1972.

———. *Frame Analysis*. New York: Harper and Row, 1974.

Gold, Peter. "Easter Sunrise Sermon." *Alcheringa/Ethnopoetics* 4 (1978):1-14.

Goldenberg, Naomi R. *Changing of the Gods*. Boston: Beacon Press, 1979.

Goldschmidt, Walter. *As You Sow*. New York: Harcourt Brace, 1947.

Goldstein, Diane E. "The Language of Religious Experience and Its Implications for Fieldwork." *Western Folklore* 42 (1983):105-13.

Goodenough, Ward. "Componential Analysis and the Study of Meaning." *Language* 32 (1956):195-216.

Goodman, Felicitas. "Phonetic Analysis of Glossolalia in Four Cultural Settings." *Journal for the Scientific Study of Religion* 8 (1969):227-39.

———. "Glossolalia: Speaking in Tongues in Four Cult Settings." *Confinia Psychiatrica* 12 (1969):113-29.

———. "Glossolalia and Hallucination in Pentecostal Congregations." *Psychiatria Clinica* 6 (1973):97-103.

———. "The Acquisition of Glossolalia Behavior." *Semiotica* 3 (1971):77-82.

———. *Speaking in Tongues*. Chicago: University of Chicago Press, 1972.

———. "The Apostolics of Yucatan: A Case Study of a Religious Movement." In *Religion, Altered States of Consciousness and Social Change*, ed. Erika Bourguignon. Columbus: Ohio State University Press, 1973.

———. "Altered Mental States vs. 'Style of Discourse'." Journal *for the Scientific Study of Religion* 11 (1972):197-99.

———, et. al., *Trance, Healing and Hallucination*. New York: John Wiley and Sons, 1974.

Gordon, Robert W. "Negro 'Shouts' From Georgia." In *Mother Wit From the Laughing Barrel*, ed. Alan Dundes, pp. 445-52. Englewood Cliffs: Prentice-Hall, 1973.

Gordon, Stanley and W.K. Bartlett and Terri Moyle. "Some Characteristics of Charismatic Experience: Glossolalia in Australia." *Journal for the Scientific Study of Religion* 3 (1964):269-78.

Gross, Larry. "Art as the Communication of Competence." *Social Science Information* 12 (1973):115-41.

Gumperz, J.J. *Language in Social Groups*. Stanford: Stanford University Press, 1971.

———. "The Speech Community." In *Language and Social Context*, ed. Pier Paolo Giglioli, pp. 219-231. New York: Penguin, 1972.

———. "Sociolinguistics and Communication in Small Groups." In *Sociolinguistics*, ed. J.B. Pride and Janet Holmes, pp. 203-24. New York: Penguin, 1972.

Hageman, Alice. *Sexist Religion and Women in the Church*. New York: Association Press, 1974.

Hallpike, C.R. "Social Hair." In *Reader in Comparative Religion*, ed. William Lessa and Evon Z. Vogt, pp. 99-105. New York: Harper and Row, 1979.

Hamilton, Michael P. *The Charismatic Movement*. Grand Rapids: Eerdmans, 1975.

Hanawalt, N.G. "Feelings of Security and of Self-esteem in Relation to Religious Belief." *Journal of Social Psychology* 59 (1963):347-53.

Harrell, David E., Jr. *All Things Are Possible: The Healing and Charismatic Revivals in Modern America*. Bloomington: Indiana University Press, 1975.

Hawkes, Terence. *Structuralism and Semiotics*. Berkeley: University of California Press, 1977.

Hawley, Florence, "The Keresan Holy Rollers." *Social Forces* 47 (1969):272-80.

Helm, June, ed. *Symposium on New Approaches to the Study of* Religion. Seattle: University of Washington Press, 1964.

———. *Essays on the Verbal and Visual Arts*. Seattle: University of Washington Press, 1967.

Hendricks, W.O. *Essays on Semiolinguistics and Verbal Art*. The Hague: Mouton, 1973.

Hill, Samuel S., ed. *Religion and the Solid South*. Nashville: Abingdon Press, 1972.

Hine, Virginia. "Pentecostal Glossolalia: Toward a Functional Interpretation." *Journal for the Scientific Study of Religion* 8 (1969):21-26.

———. "Bridge-Burners: Commitment and Participation in a Religious Movement." *Sociological Analysis* 31 (1970):61-66.

———. "Non-Pathological Pentecostal Glossolalia: A Summary of Relevant Psychological Literature." *Journal for the Scientific Study of Religion* 8 (1969):211-26.

Hoch-Smith, Judith and Anita Spring. *Women in Ritual and Symbolic Roles*. New York: Plenum Press, 1978.

Hoekema, Anthony A. *What About Tongue-Speaking*? Grand Rapids: Eerdmans, 1966.

Hollenweger, W.J. *The Pentecostals*. Minneapolis: Augsburg, 1972.

Holm, Nils G. "Ritualistic Patterns and Sound Structure of Glossolalia in Material Collected in the Swedish-speaking parts of Finland." *Temenos* 11 (1975):43-60.

Holt, Grace Sims. "Stylin' Outta the Black Pulpit." In *Rappin' and Stylin' Out*, ed. Thomas Kochman, pp. 189-205. Urbana: University of Illinois Press, 1977.

Holt, John B. "Holiness Religion: Cultural Shock and Social Reorganization." *American Sociological Review* 5 (1940):740-47.

Honko, L. "Genre Analysis in Folkloristics and Comparative Religion." *Temenos* 3 (1967):48-64.

Hultkrantz, A. "The Phenomenology of Religion: Aims and Methods." *Temenos* 6 (1970):68-88.

Hutch, Richard A. "The Personal Ritual of Glossolalia." *Journal for the Scientific Study of Religion* 19 (1980):264-81.

Hymes, Dell. "Ethnography of Speaking." In *Anthropology and Human Behavior*, ed. T. Gladwin and William Sturtevant. Washington, D.C.: Anthropological Society, 1962.

———. "Ethnography of Communication." *American Anthropologist* 66 (1964):1-34.

———. "Directions in (Ethno) Linguistic Theory." In "Transcultural Studies in Cognition." *American Anthropologist* 66 (1964):6-56.

———. "The Anthropology of Communication." In *Human Communication Theory*, ed. Frank E.X. Dance. New York: Holt, Rinehart and Winston, 1967.

———. "Sociolinguistics and the Ethnography of Speaking." In *Social Anthropology and Language*, ed. Edwin Ardener, pp. 47-94. London: Tavistock, 1971.

———. "Models of the Interaction of Language and Social Setting." *Journal of Social Issues* 23 (1967):8-28.

———. "Breakthrough into Performance." In *Folklore, Performance, and Communication*, ed. Dan Ben-Amos and Kenneth Goldstein. The Hague: Mouton, 1975.

———. *Foundations in Sociolinguistics*. Philadelphia: University of Pennsylvania Press, 1974.

———. "The Ethnography of Speaking." In *Language, Culture, and Society*, ed. Ben Blount. Cambridge: Winthrop, 1974.

———. "The Grounding of Performance and Text in a Narrative View of Life." *Alcheringa* 4 (1978):137-40.

———. *What Is Ethnography*? Austin: Southwest Educational Developmental Lab., 1978.

Jackson, George Pullen. "The 'Old-Time Religion' as a Folk Religion." *Tennessee Folklore Society Bulletin* 7 (1941):30-39.

———. *White Spirituals in the Southern Uplands*. Chapel Hill: University of North Carolina Press, 1933.

Jacobs, Sue-Ellen. *Women in Perspective: A Guide for Cross-Cultural Studies*. Urbana: University of Illinois Press, 1976.

Jain, R.K. *Text and Context: The Social Anthropology of Tradition*. Philadelphia: Institute for the Study of Human Issues, 1977.

Jakobson, Roman. "Closing Statement: Linguistics and Poetics." In *Style in Language*, ed. Thomas A. Sebeok, pp. 350-78. Cambridge: M.I.T. Press, 1960.

James, Janet W., ed. *Women in American Religion*. Philadelphia: University of Pennsylvania Press, 1976.

James, William. *The Varieties of Religious Experience*. New York: Random House, 1929.

Jansen, William "Classifying Performance in the Study of Verbal Folklore." In *Studies in Folklore*, ed. W. Edson Richmond. Bloomington: Indiana University Press, 1957.

———. "The Esoteric-Exoteric Factor in Folklore." In *The Study of Folklore*, ed. Alan Dundes. Englewood Cliffs: Prentice-Hall, 1965.

Jeffner, Anders. *The Study of Religious Language*. London: SCM Press, 1972.

Johnson, Benton. "A Framework for the Analysis of Religious Action with Special Reference to Holiness and Non-Holiness Groups." Ph.D. dissertation, Harvard University, 1953.

———. "Do Holiness Sects Socialize in Dominant Values?" *Social Forces* 39 (1961):309-16.

———. "A Critical Appraisal of the Cult-Sect Typology." *American Sociological Review* 22 (1957):88-92.

———. "On Church and Sect." *American Sociological Review* 28 (1963):539-49.

———. "Church and Sect Revisited." *Journal for the Scientific Study of Religion* 10 (1971):124-37.

Johnson, Charles. *The Frontier Camp Meeting*. Dallas: Southern Methodist University Press, 1955.

Jones, Michael O. *Why Faith Healing*? Canadian Centre for Folk Cultural Studies, No. 3, 1972.

Jordan, David K. *Gods, Ghosts and Ancestors: Folk Religion in a Taiwanese Village*. Berkeley: University of California Press, 1972.

Jorstad, Erling. *The Holy Spirit in Today's Church*. Nashville: Abington, 1973.

Kane, Steven. "Aspects of Holy Ghost Religion." Ph.D. dissertation, University of North Carolina, 1973.

———. "Holy Ghost People." *Appalachian Journal* 1:255-61.

———. "Ritual Possession in a Southern Appalachian Religious Sect." *Journal of American Folklore* 87 (1974):293-303.

Kelly, M.W. "Depression in the Psychoses of Members of the Religious Community of Women." *American Journal of Psychiatry* 118 (1962):423-25.

Kelsey, Morton. *Tongue Speaking*. New York: Doubleday, 1964.

Kendrick, K. "The Pentecostal Movement: Hopes and Hazards." *Christian Century* 80 (1963):608-10.

Kerr, Laura N. *Lady in the Pulpit*. New York: Woman's Press, 1951.

Kevelson, Roberta. "Language Games as Systematic Metaphors." *Semiotica* 19 (1977):29-37.

Key, Mary Ritchie. *Male Female Language*. New Jersey: Scarecrow Press, 1975.

Kildahl, John P. *The Psychology of Speaking in Tongues*. New York: Harper and Row, 1972.

Kochman, Thomas. "Toward an Ethnography of Black American

Speech Behavior." In *Rappin' and Stylin' Out*, ed. Thomas Kochman, pp. 241-65. Urbana: University of Illinois Press, 1977.

Knox, Ronald A. *Enthusiasm*. London: Oxford Press, 1960.

Kroll-Smith, J. Stephen. "The Testimony as Performance." *Journal for the Scientific Study of Religion* 19 (1980):16-25.

Kuhlman, Katherine. *I Believe in Miracles*. Englewood Cliffs: Prentice-Hall, 1968.

———. *God Can Do It Again*. Englewood Cliffs: Prentice-Hall, 1969.

LaBarre, Weston. "Materials for a History of Studies of Crisis Cults: A Bibliographic Essay." *Current Anthropology* 12 (1971):3-45.

———. *They Shall Take Up Serpents*. Minneapolis: University of Minnesota Press, 1962.

———. "Snake-handling Cult of the American Southeast." In *Explorations in Cultural Anthropology*, ed. Ward Goodenough. New York: McGraw Hill, 1964.

Labov, William and Joshua Waletzky. "Narrative analysis: Oral Versions of Personal Experience." In *Essays on the Verbal and Visual Arts*, ed. June Helm, pp. 12-75. Seattle: Washington University Press, 1967.

Labov, William, "The Study of Language in Its Social Context." In *Sociolinguistic Patterns*, ed. William Labov. Philadelphia: University of Pennsylvania Press, 1972.

LaFontaine, J.S. *The Interpretation of Ritual*. London: Tavistock, 1972.

Lakoff, Robin. "Language in Context." *Language* 48 (1972):907-27.

———. *Language and Woman's Place*. New York: Harper & Row, 1974.

Lamphere, Louise. "Strategies, Cooperation and Conflict Among Women in Domestic Groups." In *Woman, Culture and Society*, ed. Michelle Rosaldo and L. Lamphere, pp. 97-112. Stanford: Stanford University Press, 1974.

Laski, Marghanita. *Ecstasy: A Study of Some Religious and Secular Experiences*. Bloomington: Indiana University Press, 1961.

Lawless, Elaine J. " 'What Did She Say?' An Application of Peirce's General Theory of Signs to Glossolalia in the Pentecostal Religion." *Folklore Forum* 13 (1980):23-38.

———. "Brothers and Sisters: Pentecostals as a Folk Group." *Western Folklore 43 (1983): 85-104.*

———. "Shouting for the Lord: The Power of Women's Speech in the Pentecostal Service." *Journal of American Folklore* 96 (1983):433-57.

———. "Make a Joyful Noise: An Ethnography of Communication

in the Pentecostal Service." *Southern Folklore Quarterly* 44 (1980): 1-32.

———. " 'I Know If I Don't Bear My Testimony I'll Lose It': Mormon Women's Testimonies." *Kentucky Folklore Quarterly* 30 (1984): 32-49.

———. "Traditional Women Preachers in Mid-Missouri." *Missouri Folklore Society Journal* 6 (1984): 47-60.

———. "Oral 'Character' and 'Literary' Art: A Call for a New Reciprocity Between Oral Literature and Folklore." *Western Folklore* 45 (1985): 77-97.

———. "Tradition and Poetics: The Sermons of Women Preachers." In *A Memorial for Milman Parry*, ed. John Miles Foley. Columbus, Ohio: Slavica Press, 1987, pp. 269-312.

———. " 'Your Hair is Your Glory': Public and Private Symbology for Pentecostal Women." *New York Folklore* 12 (1986):33-49.

———. "Piety and Motherhood: Reproductive Images and Maternal Strategies of the Woman Preacher." *Journal of American Folklore* 100 (1987): 83-92.

———. "Narrative in the Pulpit: Persistent Use of *Exempla* in Vernacular Religious Contexts." *The Journal of the Midwest Modern Language Association* 20 (1988), forthcoming.

———. *Handmaidens of the Lord: Women Preachers and Traditional Religion*. Philadelphia: University of Pennsylvania Press and the American Folklore Society, 1988, forthcoming.

Lawless, Elaine J. and Elizabeth Peterson. *Joy Unspeakable*. Television documentary with Indiana University Radio and Television. John Winninger, Producer. 1981.

Leach E. "Social Geography and Linguistic Performance." *Semiotica* 15 (1975):97-97.

Lebra, Takie S. "Millenarian Movements and Resocialization." *American Behavioral Scientist* 16 (1973):195-217.

Lederer, Wolfgang. *The Fear of Women*. New York: Harcourt Brace Jovanovich, 1968.

Lee, Gary R. and Robert W. Clyde. "Religion, Socioeconomic Status, and Anomie." *Journal for the Scientific Study of Religion* 13 (1974):35-47.

Lefever, Harry G. "The Religion of the Poor: Escape or Creative Force?" *Journal for the Scientific Study of Religion* 16 (1977):225-36.

Lenski, Gerhard. "Social Correlates of Religious Interest." *American Sociological Review* 18 (1953):533-44.

Lerch, Patricia. "The Role of Women in Possession-Trance Cults in Brazil." M.A. thesis, Ohio State University, 1972.

Leslie, Charles. *Anthropology of Folk Religion*. New York: Vintage, 1960.

Lessa, William A. and Evon Z. Vogt. *Reader in Comparative Religion: An Anthropological Approach*. New York: Harper and Row, 1979.

Leuba, James H. *Psychology of Religious Mysticism*. New York: Harcourt, Brace, 1925.

Lewis, I.M. *Ecstatic Religion*. Middlesex, Eng: Penguin, 1971.

Lord, Albert. *The Singer of Tales*. New York: Atheneum, 1976; First pub. Harvard University Press, 1960.

Lovekin, Adams and H. Newton Maloney. "Religious Glossolalia: A Longitudinal Study of Personality Change." *Journal for the Scientific Study of Religion* 16 (1977):383-93.

Lovell, John. "The Social Implications of the Negro Spiritual." In *Mother Wit from the Laughing Barrel*, ed. Alan Dundes, pp. 452-64. Englewood Cliffs: Prentice-Hall, 1973.

Lowe, W. L. "Religious Beliefs and Religious Delusions: A Comparative Study of Religious Projections." *Psychoanalytic Quarterly* 13 (1944):1-15.

Luther, Gerlach P. "Pentecostalism: Revolution or Counter-Revolution?" In *Religious Movements in Contemporary America*, ed. Irving L. Zaretsky, pp. 669-700. Princeton University Press, 1974.

McDermott, R. P. and David R. Roth. "The Social Organ of Behavior: Interactional Approaches." *Annual Review of Anthropology* 7 (1978):321-45.

McDowell, John Holmes. "The Corrido of Greater Mexico as Discourse, Music and Event." In *And Other Neighborly Names*, edited by Richard Bauman and Roger D. Abrahams, pp. 44-75. Austin: University of Texas Press, 1981.

McGuire, Meredith B. "Testimony as Commitment Mechanism in Catholic Pentecostal Prayer Groups." *Journal for the Scientific Study of Religion* 16 (1977):165-69.

McNamee, John J. "The Role of the Spirit in Pentecostalism." Ph.D. dissertation, Universitat Tubingen, 1974.

McPherson, Aimee Semple. *The Holy Spirit*. Los Angeles: Challpin, 1931.

———. *Give Me My Own God*. New York: H.C. Kinsey, 1936.

———. *The Four-Square Gospel*. Echo Park, Ill: Evangelistic Association, 1946.

———. *The Story of My Life*. Hollywood: An International Correspondent's Publication, 1951.

Mackie, A. *The Gift of Tongues*. New York: G.H. Doren, 1921.

Maranda, Pierre and Elli Kongas Maranda, eds. *Structural Analysis of Oral Tradition*. Philadelphia: University of Pennsylvania Press, 1971.

Marshall, Howard Wight. " 'Keep on the Sunny Side of Life': Pattern and Religious Expression in Blue-Grass Gospel Music." *New York Folklore* 30 (1974):3-43.

Martin, Ira Jay. *Glossolalia in an Apostolic Church*. Berea, Kentucky: Berea College Press, 1960.

Marty, Martin E. *Pilgrims in Their Own Land*. New York: Penguin Books, 1984.

Marx, Gary. "Religion: Opiate or Inspiration of Civil Rights Militancy Among Negroes?" In *Research in Religious Behavior*, ed. Benjamin Beit-Hallahmi. Boston: Brooks/Cole, 1973.

Masson, Margaret. "The Typology of the Female as a Model for the Regenerate: Puritan Preaching." *Signs* 2 (1977):304-15.

May, I. Carlyle. "A Survey of Glossolalia and Related Phenomena in Non-Christian Religion." *American Anthropologist* 58 (1956):75-96.

Messenger, John C. "Folk Religion." In *Folklore and Folklife*, ed. Richard M. Dorson, pp. 217-37. Chicago: University of Chicago Press, 1972.

Miller, Terry E. "Voices From the Past: The Singing and Preaching at Otter Creek Church." *Journal of American Folklore* 88 (1975):266-82.

Minney, Robin. *Of Many Mouths and Eyes: A Study of the Forms of Religious Expression*. London: Hodder and Stoughton, 1975.

Mischel, Walter and Frances. "Psychological Aspects of Spirit Possession." *American Anthropologist* 60 (1958): 249-60.

Mitchell, Basil, ed. *The Philosophy of Religion*. London: Oxford University Press, 1971.

Morris, James. *The Preachers*. New York: St. Martin's Press, 1973.

Murphy, William P. "Oral Literature." *Annual Review of Anthropology* 7 (1978):113-36.

Neal, Sister Marie Augusta. "Women in Religion: A Sociological Perspective." *Sociological Inquiry* 45 (1975):33-39.

Nichol, John. *Pentecostalism*. New York: Harper and Row, 1966.

Noy, Dov. "Is There a Jewish Folk Religion?" In *Studies in Jewish Folklore*, ed. Frank Talmage, pp. 273-87. Cambridge, Mass: Association for Jewish Studies, 1980.

Oats, Wayne E. "A Sociopsychological Study of Glossolalia." In *Glossolalia*, ed. Frank E. Stagg. Nashville: Abington, 1967.

O'Connor, Edward D. *Perspectives on Charismatic Renewal*. London: University of Notre Dame Press, 1975.

Ortner, Sherry. "On Key Symbols." In *Reader Comparative Religion*, ed. William A. Lessa and Evon Z. Vogt, pp. 92-99. New York: Harper and Row, 1979.

———. "Is Female to Male as Nature is to Culture?" In *Woman, Culture and Society*, ed. Michelle Rosaldo and Louis Lamphere. Stanford: Stanford University Press, 1974.

Otterland, Anders and Lennart Sunnergren. *Upwinds*. Nashville: Thomas Nelson, 1975.

Paredes, Americo and Richard Bauman, eds. *Toward New Perspectives in Folklore*. Austin: University of Texas Press, 1972.

Pattison, E. Mansell. "Behavioral Scientific Research on the Nature Glossolalia." *Journal of the American Scientific Affiliation* 120:73-86.

———. "Ideological Support for the Marginal Middle Class: Faith Healing and Glossolalia." In *Religious Movements in Contemporary America*, ed. Irving L. Zaretsky, pp. 418-58. Princeton: Princeton University Press, 1974.

Pelto, Pertti J. and Gretel H. "Intracultural Diversity: Some Theoretical Issues." *American Ethnologist* 2 (1975):1-18.

Pentikainen, Juha. "Taxonomy and Source Criticism of Oral Tradition." In *Science of Religion*, ed. L. Honko. Turku, Finland, Proceedings of the Study Conference of the International Association for the History of Religions, 1973.

———. "Religio-Anthropological Depth Research." In *Folklore Today*, ed. Linda Degh, Henry Glassie and Felix Oinas, pp. 403-14. Bloomington: Indiana University Press, 1976.

Phillips, Susan. "Sex Differences and Language." *Annual Review of Anthropology* 9 (1980):523-44.

Plaskow, Judith and Joan Arnold, eds. *Women and Religion*. Scholars Press for the American Academy of Religion, 1974.

Poblette, Renato and Thomas F. Odea. "Anomie and the 'Quest for the Community': The Formation of Sects Among the Peurto Ricans of New York." *American Catholic Sociological Review* 21 (1960):18-36.

Pope, Liston. *Millhands and Preachers*. New York: Yale University Press, 1942.

Porter, Judith and Alexa A. Albert. "Subculture or Assimilation? A Cross-cultural Analysis of Religion and Women's Roles." *Journal for the Scientific Study of Religion* 16 (1977):17-29.

Porterfield, Amanda. *Feminine Spirituality in America*. Philadelphia: University of Pennsylvania Press, 1980.

Pride, J.B. and J. Holmes, eds. *Sociolinguistics*. Middlesex, Eng: Penguin, 1972.

Quinn, Naomi. "Anthropological Studies on Women's Status." *Annual Review of Anthropology* 6 (1977):181-225.

Ramsey, Ian. *Religious Language*. London: SCM Press, 1957.

Rappaport, Roy. "Concluding Comments on Ritual and Reflexivity." *Semiotica* 30 (1980):181-93.

Redfield, Robert. "The Folk Society." *American Journal of Sociology* 52 (1947):293-308.

Reiter, Rayna. *Toward an Anthropology of Women*. New York: Monthly Review Press, 1975.

Richardson, James. "Pyschological Interpretation of Glossolalia." *Journal for the Scientific Study of Religion* 12 (1973):199-207.

Rogers, Susan Carol. "Female Form of Power and the Myth of Male Dominance." *American Ethnologist* 2 (1975):727-56.

Rooth, Anna-Birgitta. "Taxonomy and the Source Criticism of Oral Tradition." In *Science of Religion*, ed. L. Honko, pp. 53-70. Turko, Finland. 1973.

Rosaldo, M.Z. "The Use and Abuse of Anthropology: Reflections on Feminism and Cross-Culture Understanding." *Signs* 5 (1980): 389-417.

Rosaldo, M.Z. and Louis Lamphere, eds. *Woman, Culture, and Society*. Stanford: Stanford University Press, 1974.

Rosenberg, Bruce. "The Oral Quality of Rev. Shegog's Sermon in William Faulkner's *The Sound and the Fury*." *Literature in Wissenschaft und Unterricht* 2 (1969):73-88.

———. "The Formulaic Quality of Spontaneous Sermons." *Journal of American Folklore* 83 (1970):3-20.

———. *The Art of the American Folk Preacher*. New York: Oxford University Press, 1970.

———. "The Psychology of the Spiritual Sermon." In *Religious Movements in Contemporary America*, ed. Irving I. Zaretsky, pp. 135-50. Princeton: Princeton University Press, 1974.

———. "Oral Sermons and Oral Narrative." In *Folklore, Performance, and Communication*, ed. Dan Ben Amos and Kenneth Goldstein. The Hague: Mouton, 1975.

Ruether, Rosemary Radford. *Religion and Sexism*. New York: Simon and Schuster, 1974.

Samarin, William *Tongues of Men and Angels*. New York: McMillan, 1972.

———. "The Linguistics of Glossolalia." *Hartford Quarterly* 8:49-75.

Sanches, M. and B. G. Blount. *Sociocultural Dimensions of Language Use*. New York: Academic Press, 1975.

Sapir, J.D. and J.C. Crocker, eds. *The Social Use of Metaphor*. Philadelphia: University of Pennsylvania Press, 1977.

Schermerhoren, R.A. "Ethnicity in the Perspective of the Sociology of Knowledge." *Ethnicity* 1 (1974):1-23.

Schwarz, Berthold. "Ordeal by Serpents, Fire and Strychnine." *Psychiatric Quarterly* 34 (1960):405-29.

Schwimmer, E.G. "Folkloristics and Anthropology." *Semiotica* 17 (1976):267-89.

Searle, J. "What is a Speech Act?" In *Language and Social Context*, ed. Pier Paola Giglioli, pp. 136-54. New York: Penguin, 1972.

Sebeok, Thomas A. *Style in Language*. Cambridge: M.I.T. Press, 1960.

Sessions, Jim and Bill Troy, special editors. "On Jordan's Stormy Banks: Religion in the South." *Southern Exposure* 4, (1976). Special issue.

Sherrill, John L. *They Speak With Other Tongues*. New York: McGraw Hill, 1964.

Slobin, D.I., ed. *A Field Manual for Acquisition of Communication Competence*. Berkeley: Language Behavior Research Lab, 1967.

Smart, N. "Interpretation and Mystical Experience." *Religious Studies* 1(1975):75-89.

Smith, Robert J. *The Art of the Festival*. Lawrence: University of Kansas Press, 1975.

Sobel, Bernard. "The M'lochim: A Study of a Religious Community." M.A. thesis, New School of Social Research, 1956.

Spender, Dale. *Man Made Language*. London: Routledge & Kegan Paul, 1980.

Spindler, George and Louise. *Dreamers Without Power: The Menomini Indians*. New York: Holt, Rinehart and Winston, 1971.

Spiro, Melford E. "Religion and the Irrational." In *Symposium on New Approaches to the Study of Religion*, ed. June Helm. Seattle: University of Washington Press, 1964.

———. "Religion: Problems of Definition and Explanation." In *Anthropological Approaches to the Study of Religion*, ed. Michael Banton, pp. 85-124. London: Tavistock, 1966.

Spretnak, Charlene. *The Politics of Women's Spirituality*. New York: Doubleday, 1982.

Stagg, Frank. *Glossolalia*. Nashville: Abingdon, 1967.

Stahl, Sandra K. D. "The Personal Narrative as Folklore." *Journal of the Folklore Institute* 14 (1977):9-30.

Stanley, Gordon, et al., "Some Characteristics of Charismatic Experience." *Journal for the Scientific Study of Religion* 17 (1978):269-78.

Stanton, Elizabeth Cady. *The Woman's Bible*. New York: Arno Press, 1974.

Stark, Rodney and William Sims Bainbridge. "American-born Sects: Initial Findings." *Journal for the Scientific Study of Religion* 20 (1981):130-49.

Stark, Rodney and Charles Glock. *American Piety: The Nature of Religious Commitment*. Berkeley: University of California Press, 1970.

Stekert, Ellen. "The Snake-handling Sect of Harlan County, Kentucky." *Southern Folklore Quarterly* 27 (1963):316-22.

———. "Focus for Conflict: Southern Mountain Medical Beliefs in Detroit." In *The Urban Experience and Folk Traditions*, ed. Americo Paredes and Ellen J. Stekert. Austin: University of Texas Press, 1971.

Stone, O. M. "Cultural Uses of Religious Visions: A Case Study." *Ethnology* 1 (1962):329-48.

Sudnow, David, ed. *Studies in Social Interaction*. Englewood Cliffs: Prentice-Hall, 1972.

Suojanen, Paivikki. "The Contribution of Socio-Linguistics to the Study of Religion." *Temenos* 10 (1974):114-23.

Sunden, H. "Psychology of Religion, An Orientation." *Temenos* 6 (1970):142-99.

Sweet, William Warren. *Religion on the American Frontier*. New York: Henry Holt, 1931.

———. *Religion in the Development of American Culture*. New York: Charles Scribners, 1952.

Synan, Vinson. *The Holiness-Pentecostal Movement in the United States*. Grand Rapids: Eerdmans, 1971.

Tedlock, Dennis. *The Spoken Word and the Work of Interpretation*. Philadelphia: University of Pennsylvania Press, 1983.

Thomas, Keith. "An Anthropology of Religion and Magic." *Journal of Interdisciplinary History* 6 (1976):42-60.

Thorne, Barrie and Nancy Henley, eds. *Language and Sex: Difference and Dominance*. Rowley, Mass: Newbury House, 1975.

Titon, Jeff and Ken George. "Testimonies: Transcribed Testimonies of Rachel Franklin, Edith Cubbage, Rev. John Sherfey." *Alcheringa/Ethnopoetics* 4 (1978):68-83.

———. "Dressed in the Armor of God." *Alcheringa/Ethnopoetics* 3 (1977):10-31.

———. "Some Recent Pentecostal Revivals: A Report in Words and Photographs." *Georgia Review* 32 (1978):579-605.

———. "Powerhouse for God: Sacred Speech, Chant, and Song in an Appalachian Baptist Church." American Folklore Recordings, ed. Daniel W. Patterson. Chapel Hill: Univ. of North Carolina Press, 1982.

Toelken, Barre. *The Dynamics of Folklore*. Boston: Houghton Mifflin, 1979.

Turner, Roy, ed. *Ethnomethodology*. Middlesex, Eng: Penguin, 1974.

Turner, Victor W. *The Ritual Process*. Chicago: Aldine, 1969.

———. "Betwixt and Between: The Liminal Period in Rites of Passage." In *Symposium on New Approaches to the Study of Religion*, ed. June Helm, pp. 4-21. Seattle: University of Washington Press, 1964.

———. *Dramas, Fields and metaphors: Symbolic Action in Human Society*. Ithaca: Cornell University Press, 1974.

Uspensky, B. A. "The Influence of Language on Religious Consciousness." *Semiotica* 10 (1974):177-81.

Van Vuuren, Nancy. *The Subversion of Women*. Philadelphia: Westminster Press, 1974.

Waardenberg, Jaques. "The Language of Religion and the Study of Religions as Sign Systems." In *Science of Religion*, ed. L. Honko, pp. 441-57. Turku: Proceedings of the Study Conference of the International Association for the History of Religion, 1973.

Warburton, T. Rennie. "Holiness Religion: An Anomaly of Sectarian Typologies." *Journal for the Scientific Study of Religion* 8 (1969):130-39.

Warner, Marina. *Alone of All Her Sex*. New York: Alfred A. Knopf, 1976.

Weber, Max, *The Sociology of Religion*. Boston: Beacon Press, 1922.

Wiegle, Marta, ed. "Women as Verbal Artists." Special Issue, *Frontiers* 3, Fall, 1978.

Weisberger, Bernard. *They Gathered at the River*. Boston: Little, Brown, 1958.

Welter, Barbara. *Dimity Convictions: The American Woman in the 19th Century*. Athens: Ohio University Press, 1976.

Whitehead, Alfred N. *Religion in the Making*. New York: MacMillan, 1927.

Wilgus, D.K. "The Negro-White Spiritual." In *Mother Wit From the Laughing Barrel*, ed. Alan Dundes, pp. 67-81. Englewood Cliffs: Prentice-Hall, 1973.

Williams, Melvin D. *Community in a Black Pentecostal Church: An Anthropological Study*. Philadelphia: University of Pennsylvania Press, 1974.

Winner, Irene P. and Thomas G. "The Semiotics of Cultural Texts." *Semiotica* 18(1981):101-56.

Wood, William *Culture and Personality Aspects of the Pentecostal Holiness Religion*. The Hague: Mouton, 1965.

Yoder, Don. "Official Religion vs. Folk Religion." *Pennsylvania Folklife* 15 (1965-66):36-52.

———. "Toward a Definition of Folk Religion." *Western Folklore* 33 (1974):2-12.

———. "Introductory Bibliography on Folk Religion." *Western Folklore* 33 (1974): 13-34.

Zaretsky, Irving I., ed. *Religious Movements in Contemporary America*. Princeton: Princeton University Press, 1974.

Zeman, J. Jay "Modality and the Peircean Concept of Belief." *Semiotica* 10 (1974):205-25.

Index